JERUSALEM

THE FUTURE OF THE PAST

MOSHE SAFDIE

HOUGHTON MIFFLIN COMPANY

BOSTON

1989

Library of Congress Cataloging-in-Publication Data

Safdie, Moshe, date.
    Jerusalem : the future of the past / Moshe Safdie.
        p.   cm.

    ISBN 0-395-35375-0

    1. Architecture — Jerusalem.   2. Architecture — Jerusalem —
Conservation and restoration.   3. Jerusalem — Buildings, structures,
etc.   I. Title.

NA1478.J4S24   1989   88-32271
720′.95694′4 — dc19   CIP

Illustrations :   Moshe Safdie.
Design : Optimum Publishing Inc., Montreal.
Published in Canada by
Optimum Publishing Inc., Montreal.

Printed and bound in Canada

To Michal, daughter of Jerusalem

ACKNOWLEDGMENTS

This book has been a long time in the making. The first draft was completed in 1982. As in the case of *Beyond Habitat* and *Form and Purpose*, I produced it with the assistance of John Kettle through the edited transcription of our conversations. However, by 1985, with my decision to postpone the publication of the book, John Kettle was off to his thriving career as a futurist, and events surrounding the projects in the book suggested a comprehensive rewrite and update. In 1987, I completed redrafting the book. My close friend of twenty years, Canadian filmmaker Paul Almond, agreed to assist me with editing following an enthusiastic first reading of the manuscript. Thus I am indebted to John Kettle for helping with the birth of this book and to Paul Almond for its rebirth in current form. Thanks are also due to my friend Ada Karmi Melamede, who reviewed the manuscript and to Harry Foster of Houghton Mifflin, Laurel Sullivan and Michael Baxendale of Optimum, who worked with me throughout the preparation of the final version.

CONTENTS

To love anew is like the dilemma
Of architects in an old city: to build
Once more in places which had been
So they might look of that time, yet of today.

Yehuda Amichai

INTRODUCTION

The Old City of Jerusalem is bound by two deep valleys, Hinnom and Kidron, which separate it from the surrounding hills. It is encircled now by hotels, a university, and apartments of modern Jerusalem. From Mount Scopus and the Mount of Olives, and from the built-over hill to the west, you can look down on the Old City, a peninsula jutting out from the main plateau, where the road runs north to Nablus and on to Damascus.

It is a gold city. Jerusalem the Golden is the Jerusalem of yellow-gold limestone. I know of no city with quite that color of stone, which is made more intensely golden by the clear air, strong sun and deep blue sky.

Jerusalem has a sensual skyline. Out of the strong framework of the city walls rise two great domes, the Dome of the Rock and the al-Aksa mosque, one golden, the other silver, along with hundreds more domes of varied shapes. There are large ones on the Holy Sepulchre and other churches and small ones over the houses. There are circular, oval, elliptical and vaulted domes. Among them are the city's towers, the minarets, the spires of the churches and of Augusta Victoria. In the main, however, the texture of Jerusalem is soft and feminine. Where you would normally think of the fabric of a city as being made up of buildings standing along the edges of streets, it would be more accurate to think of Old Jerusalem as a mass of intricately carved stone. It is as if nature had deposited a solid layer of limestone three or four storeys high which followed the curves and contours of the landscape. Then, with a chisel, man cut away alleys, passages, stair ramps, courtyards and terraces.

The streets of Jerusalem are narrow — eight feet wide, twelve feet at the most. Except for the suqs, the principal markets, which still follow the alignment of the main Roman roads, the streets are never straight but continually turn and twist. Many are bridged over by rooms, built by people looking for extra space. Their windows look down onto the street. But most of the visible surfaces are solid. The openings are few — pairs of windows here and there. When you look out over the Old City, eight parts of what you see is solid walls and only two parts is openings. In a few places there are larger openings, but they are usually recessed behind arches so that light and heat are brought in frugally. The small scale and fine texture of this densely populated layer of limestone contrast strongly with occasional dark green eruptions of cypresses and pine trees.

There is a dramatic transformation as you move into the alleys and markets. In contrast to the glaring reflected sunlight that hits you as you look down on the city, the alleys are a world of shadows. The darkness is pierced by occasional dusty shafts of light blazing through tiny openings in the vaults above the markets or between the buildings, catching here a mound of plums or grapes, there a pile of silverware and copper or the glittering metal of the ironsmith. And within all that shade and coolness is another world. Here are the

Mediterranean smells of sesame paste and olive oil being ground in the mills; of the spice cumin, so common in the region's cooking; of round loaves baking with sesame seeds; of meat grilled on skewers over burning wood or charcoal; of deep-fried falafel — they chase you through the streets in waves. And then, as you come to a courtyard opening out of the narrow network of alleys, there is the sudden smell of jasmine.

Jerusalem forms a human mosaic. In the Old City you start with the great diversity of native people. There are Armenian priests in their black robes and black pointed hoods; members of Roman Catholic orders, some with brown gowns, some with gray, mostly bareheaded; Ethiopians, black-skinned, in black robes and square hats; imams with their white turbans and light robes; Hasidic Jews with their fur-rimmed hats and black coats; Sephardic rabbis, often bearded but without sidelocks, always dressed in black; Arabs in traditional dress, women with their heavily embroidered dresses, the men with the kaffiyehs and galabiehs; then the more modern Arab women in jeans and blouses but always retaining a touch of the traditional; and civilian Israelis, some in suits and ties but most dressed in slacks and open-necked shirts; and the soldiers in uniform, with slung rifles or submachine guns, some dark, others blond with blue eyes, or even redheaded. It takes some time for the visitor to distinguish between Jew and Arab. Indeed even native Jerusalemites find it harder to tell the difference as dress becomes similar and haircuts the same. One is frequently mistaken.

And then there are the pilgrims and tourists: old ladies from Greece, dressed in black, their belongings wrapped in cloth, walk around in groups; the typical American tourists, armed with two cameras, wear loud shirts, and blue and white hats bought in tourist shops; large groups of Christian pilgrims from Switzerland, France and Italy stroll about, their guides shouting a running commentary in the best accent of their native land; Israeli school children from different parts of the country come with their teachers on pilgrimage; Scandinavian and Dutch youth, their hair sun-bleached, their skin tanned, wearing shorts and backpacks, drift from hostel to hostel. U.N. soldiers from peace-keeping forces visit Jerusalem too: tall, uniformed Senegalese, Finns, Norwegians, Canadians. From time to time there are real surprises, such as groups of Japanese walking around with the blue Star of David woven on their shirts, claiming to be members of one of the ten lost tribes.

As the people of the city look different, they also move differently: the Hasidic Jews stride along with nervous energy; the farmers, with produce on their heads, sway like camels through the markets; the tourists loiter; the priests pace slowly; the children scamper.

In the markets, sounds of donkeys swinging their bells, the warning "hola" of their drivers trying to clear the way, and, always, the voices of the merchants, echo off the hard stone surfaces. As you move out of the main markets the sounds change to the cries of playing children and barking dogs. They change again as the hours go by. The roosters begin at three in the morning, and the donkeys bray in reply. Over these domestic sounds yet another layer forms; at sunrise the cacophony of religious ritual begins and washes out all other sounds. Dozens of muezzins call the city's Muslims to prayer five times a day from all the minarets. As they echo over the roofs, they create an uncomposed fugue of the highest order. The bells of the churches ring too. And as one moves toward the southeast corner of the Old City and the Western Wall, the sounds of praying become louder. This sound changes, too — from the sound of singing and the piercing cry of women on Mondays and Thursdays as bar mitzvahs or other festive occasions are celebrated to the wailing and moaning from just before Rosh Hashanah, the New Year, until Yom Kippur, the Day of Atonement, when Jews beg forgiveness.

But by far the most beautiful moments for me in Jerusalem are when the golden-hued city glows at dusk and the sounds of church bells ringing, the muezzins chanting, and Jews praying at the Wall, all blend together. As they intermingle with the sounds of the street, and as you stand anywhere in the city, you will find yourself listening to a wonderful symphony.

One cannot build with indifference in Jerusalem. It requires either an act of arrogance — building boldly as Solomon and Herod did — or of aggression — demolishing the old fabric and building anew as the Romans and Umayyads did; or it demands humility — absorbing the past, reflecting upon it, respecting it, as one considers the present and future.

CHAPTER 1

MY RETURN

The last few days before Expo opened in April of 1967 were a mad rush. Finishing touches were still being added to Habitat — grass was being laid, trees planted, and the last pieces of furniture were still coming in. And then, on opening day, there it was, my first major building, finished. By the next morning 30,000 people a day were streaming through.

Three days later, I moved with Nina, my first wife, and our two children, into one of the Habitat apartments. There around us, in three dimensions, in real materials, was everything I had lived with on paper for all those years. Here I was actually in the bathroom I had designed to be moulded from one sheet of fiber glass. After all those months of going to the workshop, building the mock-up, testing the materials, changing the forms, changing the soapdish — all of a sudden there I was, sitting in that tub and having a bath.

On the roof terrace, we could watch the sun set over the Montreal skyline, surrounded by a garden filled with lush plants, watered by the sprinkler system, morning and night. All this had been just lines on paper and now I was living in it and it was actually working. Neighbours were coming by and saying hello and telling me how much they loved living there.

It was a bit like living in the midst of a party. We were not in the south section, which was open to the public, but somehow, curious Expo visitors got through the barriers. They even walked right into our apartment, thinking it was another exhibit. With the enthusiastic public response and the press coverage in journals all over the world, I almost felt as if I were on exhibit.

But the publicity brought inquiries about my services and even offers of commissions: a developer in Puerto Rico called about building a major housing prototype using the Habitat system; the *Washington Post* architectural critic, Wolf Von Eckardt, arranged for me to meet the U.S. Secretary of Housing and Urban Development to discuss a prototype Habitat in Washington; the student council of San Francisco State College invited me to talk to them about designing their student union.

There was a steady stream of official visitors and as part of the Expo family, I was constantly involved: I showed Nelson Rockefeller around; Indira Gandhi stopped by; Charles de Gaulle spent the night at Habitat. There was an endless flood of journalists, ranging from architectural critics to fashion writers. I was involved with a lot of these activities, and I knew there was an element of self-indulgence in it.

But with the passage of summer came a sense of transition. I began investigating the offers I had received, and I travelled to the sites. My office was changing. For a couple of years, some forty architects and engineers had come from all over to work on Habitat and now they were drifting back to their homes. Obviously I had to go on to new things myself.

One bit of unfinished business in my life was my feeling for Israel. I had left my homeland at the age of 15, when my parents emigrated to Canada. Had I gone back while at university, the Israeli conscription laws would have disrupted my studies. I had made myself the promise that as soon as I completed my education, I would return and enlist for the required military service. But, after getting my degree in architecture at McGill, there was the opportunity to work for Louis Kahn, then there was Expo and the Expo master plan, and finally Habitat. I still had not returned.

In May of 1967, tension had begun to mount in the Middle East as Nasser moved Egyptian troops into the Sinai and demanded that the U.N. remove their peacekeeping forces (a demand acceded to by the U.N. Secretary-General, U Thant). Moshe Dayan was brought in as Defense Minister and it became clear that the threat to Israel was very real. Then on June 5, at the height of Expo, the Six Day War broke out.

That morning, I called the Israeli Consul General and said that I wanted to go back. For those of us outside of Israel, it was the first time we felt that the existence of the state was threatened. He said they were taking only people who were trained soldiers but in a few days untrained people like myself might be required. Would I please stand by?

But by the third day, it became clear that the tide of the war was turning and by the sixth day it was over. I was much relieved. Nonetheless, my absence from the country in which I had been born and raised continued to bother me.

The Israeli press was writing about Habitat and the Israeli-born architect who had designed it. One of the newspapers, *Ha'aretz*, featured the story in its weekend magazine. (Years later when I met Michal, who is now my wife, she remembered me as the Israeli on the *Ha'aretz* cover. She wondered as a child why an Israeli would be working abroad and not in Israel.)

As Expo was nearing its end in September 1967, the phone call I had been subconsciously hoping for finally came: Arieh Sharon, an eminent elder statesman of Israeli architecture, was inviting me to be keynote speaker at an international congress of architects and engineers in December. So just six weeks after Expo closed its gates, I was on a plane bound for Israel.

As the eastern coast of the Mediterranean came into view I found myself becoming more and more anxious. The tension grew as we flew low over Tel Aviv and circled the orange groves and the kibbutzim and villages, approaching Lod Airport. I could hardly wait to step onto Israeli soil.

But as I walked up to the terminal, I received the first of many shocks: it seemed to me like the airport of a small town in some developing country. I had a memory of everything being white, pristine, clean and elegant. My recurring dream of shiny, curved white walls, cantilevered balconies, elegant horizontal strip windows, all lush with greenery, was shattered by the reality. Everywhere I looked I saw dilapidated plaster walls with the rusting reinforcing bars showing through and makeshift structures clumsily tacked on to other buildings.

Later, when I made the very special trip back to Haifa, the port city of my boyhood, my reactions were similar. This remembered utopia of spotlessly clean white Bauhaus structures, adorned with green pines and palms, turned out to be a rather nice hillside city, not in much better condition than Naples, with lots of peeling stucco. The buildings were more run down, smaller in scale, the streets narrower, the buses shabbier, emitting more diesel smoke than I ever thought possible. What a shock to be in my sleepy home town on the eastern Mediterranean, having come to think of it over fifteen years as a paradisiacal garden of white modern structures on the hillside!

And all across Israel, I was to have the same rude awakening. The cities had grown, the suburbs had multiplied and now they were the very last word in bureaucratic architecture: row after row of four storey apartment buildings set on columns, with paved parking lots between them. I was shocked by the uglinesss and sterility of these stereotyped new suburbs.

At Lod Airport, I passed through Customs and Immigration with a clamouring, varied mass of humanity. German professors stood next to Hasidic Jews, Arab peasants next to Moroccan Jews — dark, blonde, black, all of them exuberant and excited.

Again, what a change. I had left soon after the founding of the state when mass immigration had just begun. By now the population had increased by two million and a large percentage of the new residents were Jews from Arab countries. Sephardic Jews were a much greater presence. Having grown up as one of the small Sephardic minority in Haifa and having been the only Sephardi in my class of Ashkenazim at the Reali School, I was not indifferent to this demographic shift.

Ashkenazim are those Jews whose ancestry can be traced to the Jews rounded up and exiled to Rome after the destruction of the Second Temple in A.D. 70. When the Vandals sacked Rome in A.D. 455, these Jews spread throughout Europe, first to Germany and then to Poland, and on into Russia, retaining their Judaic heritage. They developed Yiddish, based on German, as their language.

Sephardic Jews are the descendants of those Jews who left Spain at the time of the Inquisition ("Sephardi" being the Hebrew word for Spanish) and travelled mostly to North Africa, the Middle East and to Turkey and other parts of the Ottoman Empire. However, the term Sephardic also applies to those who were exiled after the destruction of the First Temple in 586 B.C. to Babylonia, Persia and other parts of the region, now Syria, Iraq, Iran, and the Yemen — in other words, to all Middle Eastern Jews, including some from India.

Although my mother was born in Manchester and has all the attributes of a Mancunian (all the way down to her Lancashire accent), her parents came to Manchester from Aleppo at the turn of the century, and so she considers herself an Aleppian. Further back, her family traces itself to the Inquisition (in Spain) and is Sephardic in the literal sense.

My father's family is assumed to have originated in the Middle East because the name Safdie means "from the town of Safad" in Galilee, where a Jewish community thrived from Roman times on down through the Ottoman period. At some point during the last couple of hundred years, my father's family moved to Aleppo, where they must have taken the name Safdie. There were also reasons for believing my father's family originated in Spain, as my father himself thought. We did not speak Ladino (the Spanish dialect of Sephardic families) but we always kept certain customs such as lighting an extra (ninth) candle in the festival of Chanuka — a tradition unique to those Jews persecuted during the Inquisition.

I arrived at the congress to find the world's most famous architects there: Louis Kahn, whom I had once worked for and much admired; Philip Johnson; and Buckminster Fuller, to name a few. This was more than just another architectural congress — it was a kind of tribute to Israel from the architects and engineers of the world. In December 1967 Israel's popularity was at its height. Almost everybody considered the Six Day War to have been a just war; most of the world seemed to recognize it as a small country's desperate fight for survival; no one accused Israel of being expansionist. The fact that Israel gained the West Bank, the eastern part of Jerusalem, the Sinai, the Gaza Strip and the Golan Heights was an unexpected side effect.

If Israel was having its triumph, at a personal level I was certainly having mine. There was enormous popular enthusiasm for Habitat. Fifty million people came to Expo and it seemed as if every one of them had gone to Habitat. And there I was, a homecoming Israeli, being received at the age of 29 by some of the great architects of the world as well as by my Israeli colleagues.

In my keynote speech I spoke with a good deal of optimism about harnessing technology to build a habitable environment as I had done with Habitat. This world of growing population densities and bureaucracies could produce a very negative environment, but it need not be that way, I maintained. In December of 1967 I believed anything could be done. I also believed that everything was going to be easy, because Habitat had been so complicated that anything else in the future would have to be relatively simple.

On the day after my keynote speech, a young woman from the Ministry of Housing asked me if I could meet the Minister, Mordechai Bentov, for lunch at the Hilton. It was my first contact with an Israeli government official, but the meeting was to have an extraordinary long term significance for me.

I found Bentov's personality and history compelling. Among my childhood memories is an image of the founding fathers of Israel, the generation of men and women who built the country. Mostly from Eastern Europe or from Germany, they were highly cultured, idealistic, passionate about the country and indifferent to their own material success. Their skills and talents could have made them wealthy yet they lived on kibbutzim (communes) or in modest apartments in the city, devoting themselves to building Israel.

They were the first generation to speak Hebrew as a modern language. Hebrew had long been the language of Jewish prayer, but when they returned to Israel they decided to make it a living language, the language of Israel. (The man most responsible was Eliezer Ben-Yehuda, whose name adorns one of the main Jerusalem streets.) Many of the early comers spoke their own languages. The Ashkenazim spoke Yiddish but the Sephardim did not. Hebrew was part of their common cultural heritage and it became the first (followed by Arabic and English) official language of Israel, which it remains today.

As Bentov walked up to the table in the Hilton where I was waiting for him, I was struck by his amazing youthfulness. Tall, thin and strong, he was then in his late sixties, a man whose tanned face and hands were those of a farmer but with the white hair and fiery blue-grey eyes of a revolutionary. Bentov came to Israel from Poland in the third wave of immigration right after the First World War, and he was part of a group of young people who founded one of the very early (and mostly left-wing) kibbutzim, Mishmar Ha'emek, in the fertile Valley of Jezreel.

Bentov immediately evoked in me memories of those rugged people of the land, people who always tread solidly, who do not express emotions. You never quite know what they are feeling; and their laughter is never whole-hearted. There is an intensity about their eyes; they have the rebellious eyes of people who are deeply committed, who have worked hard to turn their arid settlements into gardens of paradise.

Bentov looked the kibbutznik, even down to his dress. He was wearing, as always, an open white shirt, the uniform of his generation which rarely wear ties, even to official events of state.

If my fantasy of Haifa had crumbled, in this meeting another fantasy had become a reality. Mordechai Bentov confirmed the truth of the myth of the founding fathers.

As we sat there in the Hilton restaurant, with a couple of his aides, he expressed his admiration for Habitat and my work in general. Israel was facing an enormous need for new towns, new suburbs; the institutional and stereotyped character of much of the recent housing displeased him. In the 1950s and 1960s immigration had been constantly rising and poor quality projects had been built simply to give people shelter.

Now, toward the end of the 1960s, Bentov felt the country could start dealing with the issues of quality — the quality of life in the community. The country had a severe labor shortage. He was interested in the technologies we had applied and developed in Habitat. He was planning a trip to the United States shortly. Could he come to Montreal and see Habitat?

Not long after I returned to Montreal, Bentov's telegram came informing me of his arrival date.

I had always felt that the best time to see Habitat was on a beautiful sunny day in late spring or fall, when the blue sky contrasted with the beige concrete, and the gardens were lush with trees and climbers, Boston ivy and flowers planted by the tenants. As luck and the seasons would have it, the Israeli Minister of Housing arrived in January.

I met him at the airport with the Israeli Consul General, in one of the worst January snowstorms that I can recall. We kept wondering whether the plane would land at all. Eventually it touched down, we greeted him at the gate, and rushed into the black official car for the drive to Habitat.

As we turned into the driveway, Habitat looked surrealistic. The snow was blowing horizontally through the apertures between the boxes, and the flurries seemed to be enveloping the building itself. In this northern white-out, the top ends of the grey concrete mass faded into the billowing snow, so Habitat looked much bigger than it was. It might have gone on for a hundred floors and ten miles.

I was a little concerned because one of the criticisms of Habitat was that it was designed for a temperate climate, and not for a Canadian winter. Critics were fond of asking, "Why have so much open space, external surface, and open walkways in a cold climate?" (But when a survey asked the residents, "Would you prefer the pedestrian walkways to be totally enclosed and glazed?" four out of five opted for the open walkways.)

We got out of the car, and I escorted Bentov through the blizzard on a quick walking tour, even going into units to talk with the tenants. We went along the open walkways and looked down at the playgrounds, though of course there were no children playing. It must have been 20 degrees below zero. But blizzard or not, he was impressed.

Later we sat in one of the apartments and discussed how we could build a similar project in Israel.

We discussed taking the technological ideas of prefabrication devised for Habitat and introducing them on a wide scale in Israel. It would entail putting together a team of technical people who knew prefabrication and bringing them over. And even more difficult, the team would have to collaborate with their Israeli counterparts. Local contractors and manufacturers would have to be convinced that these techniques were worth trying, and I knew from Habitat that this would not be an easy task.

We would have to set up factories in several parts of the country and choose locations where the road system permitted transportation of modules four metres wide.

My proposal to the ministry would eventually have to include designs for gigantic molds, production facilities, assembly lines for the components, a study of the shipping logistics, and an actual design to show how the system would be applied on the first site — what kind of apartments, what kind of building clusters, even what kind of parking arrangements.

At the conclusion of the meeting, Bentov invited me to begin working on a proposal which I would present to the Director General of the Ministry of Housing, Max Taneh.

This was not just a commission to choose a site and make a design. What we were discussing was a design plus a means of production: whole factories, assembly lines, molds, special manufacturing of bathrooms, kitchens, windows, and so on . . . I was overwhelmed and exhilarated.

MY KIBBUTZ

Although I grew up in a city, by age eleven my friends and I had joined youth movements — the scouts, HaShomer Hatza'ir and other groups — with the idea that at age eighteen we would join the army as a group and thereafter form a kibbutz in the country. Summer work camps in a kibbutz would give us a first-hand taste of that life. So at the age of fourteen, my friends and I spent the summer on Kibbutz Neot Mordecai, north of the Sea of Galilee.

I have since come to realize that the physical appearance of a kibbutz is very much a manifestation of the particular stage in its evolution as a social entity. Neot Mordecai was a young kibbutz. Rows of one storey wood huts served as residences for the adults; there was only one small room per individual or couple. There were slightly larger huts for the children with makeshift bunk beds. The huts were all quite close together and linked by a curvilinear path. The dining room was centrally located and was the focus of social life; all of us ate all our meals there. Larger sheds housed poultry, cattle and the agricultural machinery. Since we were a young kibbutz, our vegetation was also immature, scrawny trees and struggling sunburned grass.

The highlight of each day for my friends and me was the visit to the communal shower which most of the kibbutz members used because it had hot water. The women's and men's showers were separated by a thin wall. Strategically located holes were drilled providing us with an illicit first full view of our female companions and the more mature kibbutz ladies.

The kibbutz was relatively small, perhaps one-hundred and fifty members. It was poor and the work was hard — almost all of it in agriculture. Clothing was very uniform: men with khaki slacks, shorts in summer, skirts for women only on special occasions.

Twenty years later I returned to Neot Mordecai. Some of the wood sheds were still there, almost invisible under the lush trees, and children still lived in separate residences. However, most members now lived in two storey duplex units (four families per house with a central staircase). They not only had their own showers but also little kitchenettes too. Lunch, the main meal, was still eaten in the communal dining room, but morning and evening meals were often cooked at home. The staggered two storey concrete and stucco buildings with their red tile roofs were separated by lavish plantlife and surrounded a luxurious dining room with glassed-in areas looking onto the common green. Beyond were new large buildings for industrial production. Within the cycle of thirty years, the austere, almost unfurnished rooms of my kibbutz had evolved into petit bourgeois, individually furnished suites, complete with television and stereo sound.

The early kibbutzim are now wonderfully landscaped with lawns, boulevards of great palm trees, bougainvillea and jasmine. Several of the living quarters are being expanded to add bedrooms for the children, who can now live with their parents. However, older members still live in their one storey huts made of wood and, indeed, the average age has increased in most kibbutzim and care of the elderly is now a major problem. Living conditions are still modest but industries have developed and a great deal of wealth has been accumulated. In fact, this wealth has created new problems. Should they hire laborers? Should kibbutzim bring in outside people for wages? Should these idealistic and very communally minded people now become bourgeois employers?

CHAPTER 2

HABITAT JERUSALEM

I began working on developing a Habitat for Israel immediately. I gathered together a small group of four or five engineers and production experts; some had been involved with Habitat Montreal, others had worked on Habitat Puerto Rico and had developed a new concrete technology, expanding self-stressing concrete. We made contacts with Israeli manufacturers who were anxious to join forces with us and began to work out the technical details. This work went on for several months, during which time I went to Israel about once a month, often bringing one or two engineers with me.

Work sessions with the Ministry and with potential partners for the production facilities went extremely well. After a while, one learns to differentiate between projects that have official backing, in which everything works and works fast, and projects that are done in spite of the bureaucracy, in which everything becomes an impossibility and nothing goes smoothly. For now, we had the kind of open-door, red-carpet treatment that is given to a project with official sanction, and I felt that the new Habitat would soon be under construction.

All the logic pointed us towards Jerusalem as the first location. Meeting with Mayor Teddy Kollek may have unconsciously affected my choice. His dynamism inspires confidence and his enthusiasm is contagious. I first met him on the final day of the 1967 architectural congress when we all moved up to Jerusalem. A tour of the city was organized, and we then met with the Mayor. As we toured, he spoke of his hopes and dreams for the city, of what had been done and what he intended to do. Everyone there had heard much about Teddy, though in 1967 his fame as Mayor was yet to rise. He was known as that "cultured Viennese," founding member of Kibbutz Ein Gev on the Sea of Galilee, director general of Ben Gurion's office; the man who set up the Tourist Office; the man who invented, created, raised funds for and built the Israel Museum. What was clear was that here was a man who cared for the heritage of the city, who was genuinely interested in advice from others, and with whom it would be a pleasure to work. That, combined with my love for the city, its villages, its valleys and hills made it clear that Jerusalem was the place to build the next Habitat.

Much construction was going on in Tel Aviv and on the outskirts of Haifa but I sensed that Jerusalem was going to be the area of real growth, having just been reunited as a result of the Six Day War. But beyond the promise of growth, I was altogether captivated by the city. I came to feel that I wanted to build there and no place else.

We began to look for actual sites around Jerusalem. The search took me from one large parcel of government-held land to another, until we arrived at Manchat just outside of Jerusalem. The Manchat hill jutted almost like a peninsula, with its elongated ridge stretching into the valleys that surrounded it. On the ridge was a charming Arab village. I was at once captivated by the site and equally impressed with its fragility and sensitivity to new development. My urge to

build here would force me to relate the new to the old, to have the project coexist with the village. The risks were enormous.

When an architect chooses a vacant site, he knows that anything he does will stand on its own. And he has his own criteria to evaluate what he has designed. Here, not only would my buildings be compared with the charm and beauty of the indigenous village, but the appropriateness was bound to become a public issue.

The traces of the retaining walls of the terraced agriculture of biblical times were dotted with more recent almond and olive trees. Here and there were rock outcroppings, some containing ancient burial places. To one side of the hill sat the village, its delicate structure of stone buildings, vaults and domes spiralling upwards, terrace upon terrace, to the summit where, quite appropriately, toward the east, there stood a Muslim stone mosque and minaret.

Here was a prototype, the ancient village, with which any modern development would have to coexist. Could one put a ten storey building next to it? Or one made of glass?

There were still more profound questions: the village represented a way of life, a certain mode of developing the land, a way of integrating construction into the landscape, establishing the privacy of the family in the context of the village, and the identity of the village as a community. The challenge of matching this declaration of values in our new construction was overwhelming.

There was also the issue of historic preservation. Much of Manchat had been taken over by Jewish refugees in 1948 following the flight of Palestinians during the War of Independence. It was now a beautiful, charming semi-slum, with families living in crowded rooms.

Hill sites make more exciting environments than flat plains, and this was another reason I was attracted to Manchat. If one builds two storey buildings on a hill, every unit has a view and looks out into the distance, whereas on a flat site they become internalized. I don't think it's an accident that wherever there is a choice, indigenous buildings in the eastern Mediterranean are built on hills. This preserved the flat fertile land for cultivation but there were other equally compelling environmental reasons. The hill was defensible, definable, and the optimal orientation could be chosen: for example, the south side, which gets the most sun in winter. The overall design of Habitat had resulted from similar considerations except that in Habitat the hill was hollow. And here, in a somewhat dilapidated form, were the roots from which Habitat had sprung — in the way of life and values Manchat embodied. I was being challenged to relate the new Habitat in Jerusalem to the traditions of its villages.

We began by making a model of the entire hill. I always start with models. I wanted a model that would show the shape of the buildings and how they would fit into the Manchat landscape. From this model, I developed a plan for a community that was akin to an Arab village in the sense that it followed the hill, each unit had its roof garden, and a series of pathways followed the topography intimately. It was certainly a very different kind of environment from the superblocks built by the Ministry.

As I immersed myself more deeply into understanding the village, I began also to understand, at the most fundamental level, the difference in attitude between its untrained indigenous builders and contemporary architects. The traditional city interweaves paths and public spaces, roots and arteries, habitations and institutions, all delicately juxtaposed, forming a continuum.

But after World War I, possibly in reaction to the overcrowding and utilitarian sameness of workers' row housing, various architects, including those of the Bauhaus and Le Corbusier, developed a whole range of supposed utopias: the Ville Radieuse of Le Corbusier, the Glass Towers in the Park of Mies van der Rohe, as well as notions (developed in Holland, Germany and Vienna) of model communities as clusters of detached buildings, set free in the landscape, juxtaposed against each other as soldiers in a field. Out of these came the idea of the city as a giant abstract sculpture, with elements now on the scale of mountains or giant towers — experienced at great distances or traversed at great speeds in the brave new world of modern transportation.

These are cities imagined in abstract and intellectual terms, rather than cities emerging from the compassionate search for the way people live their private and public lives. To me, they look more like objects created by supermen than habitations made by little animals, boring in the hill, making their own nests, or beehives, or houses in trees.

While continuing our work on Manchat, Bentov and I soon discovered another common interest and concern. We were both advocates of reconciliation with the Palestinians. Immediately after the Six Day War in 1967, Bentov had initiated a plan to build new Arab settlements on the West Bank and to provide permanent housing and employment for some of the Palestinian refugees. I had long been concerned with the problem and had, during my apprenticeship in 1962 with Louis Kahn, drawn up a proposal for a model refugee community to be constructed in Giza, near the Egyptian pyramids. In retrospect, it was an arrogant proposal, considering the location, and it was naive in assuming the Palestinians would happily settle in Egypt, or that the Egyptians would let them settle there. It is now my belief that no real solution to the problem of the Palestinians will be found outside Palestine. One way or another, the Palestinians and the Israelis will both have to live on this land that each calls home.

Then, in 1967, the entire West Bank came under Israeli control, making it possible for new Arab settlements to be constructed there and also on the Gaza Strip, where refugees lived in large numbers. In England, Baron Edmond de Rothschild was actively working to find international funds to back the construction. Bentov had initiated contact with him and thought I should go to London to meet him.

My first encounter with the Baron took place at the Rothschild Bank building in the financial district. As my taxi drove past St. Paul's Cathedral and through the more densely packed streets of the "city", it was difficult not to feel excited. I was going to meet the direct descendant of the Nadiv (Hebrew for Great Benefactor), who had pioneered and financed the modern settlement of Jews in Palestine. One of the principal streets in my home town, Haifa, was named Rothschild Boulevard — as was the case in almost every city in Israel.

The Rothschild Bank is on a narrow alley; it is an undistinguished limestone extension between two older buildings, dated circa 1950. But for "N.M. Rothschild" in brass letters on the left, it has a strange anonymity: the centre of an enormous international banking empire, housed in a nondescript building very easy to miss.

Inside the door, the modern touch disappears; the walls are covered with portraits of generations of Rothschilds. I was taken through plush corridors, all wood-panelled and very quietly carpeted, into a well worn office, comfortable with the feeling of an English country house. And there was Rothschild.

I don't know quite what I expected of a legend, but my first surprise was his kind and jovial manner. He wore a loose, soft, double-breasted suit and there was a rosiness in his cheeks. Slightly plump, with a relaxed smile and greying hair, he immediately put me at ease, talking about common acquaintances and of course about the reason for our meeting — the Palestinian refugee problem. It was the opportunity of a generation. He seemed pleased with my own interest and commitment and we talked in general terms about how we might cooperate.

I recognized that the return of Palestinians to Israel from Jordan and Lebanon could be handled only within the framework of a peace treaty, but I felt that something could be done immediately. We could remove the stigma felt by the refugees now living in the West Bank or Gaza by building permanent new towns for them and simultaneously establishing industries that would generate jobs and a stronger economy. The concept was similar to the Israeli development towns where Jewish refugees, mostly from Arab countries, had been settled in new cities in the Negev and the Galilee, with key industries strategically placed to generate jobs.

He agreed with me, adding that we could even use the same fund-raising techniques employed by the Jewish community abroad to generate the vast amount of money needed. This could demonstrate Israel's commitment to resolve the problem and also defuse the Palestinian antagonism, which was being exacerbated by the dreadful conditions in the refugee camps.

Rothschild was involved at that time with financing the Churchill Falls power project in Labrador, so he frequently came to

Montreal. He would be there in three weeks — could we meet then and perhaps map out a strategy? Thus began a series of meetings at the Ritz Carlton in Montreal. In summer the dining room opens up into an elegant garden, where we dined and talked.

Rothschild's and Bentov's interest brought others into the project: Shimon Peres, then Israeli Minister of Transport but also with special responsibility for the occupied areas; Shlomo Gazit, then coordinator of government operations in the occupied territories; Baruch Yekutieli who was a director of Bank Leumi and one of the country's foremost economic thinkers.

These influential men helped the refugee project gain momentum. I proposed setting up housing factories to be used first to build the new communities and then to supply prefabricated components for housing throughout the region. I travelled all over the West Bank looking for sites. I visited refugee camps and met various Arab community leaders. Some expressed reservations, but on the whole, their reactions were surprisingly positive.

But then came the first of two jolting setbacks. First, Prime Minister Levi Eshkol decided to squelch the whole idea. He maintained that until there was a full peace treaty between Israel and all its Arab neighbors, Israel should not take unilateral action in the matter of the Palestinian refugees. We were incredulous and thought his decision was tragically short-sighted. First, it did not recognize the uniqueness of the moment, the exuberance that followed the Six Day War and the confusion of the Palestinians. The situation was still fluid, with attitudes not yet entrenched. The Palestinians on the West Bank didn't quite know how to respond to the Israeli presence, and the extreme nationalists on both sides were not as organized as they later became. I felt strongly that what was then possible might become impossible a few years later. Unfortunately recent events have proved that to be right. What a great opportunity was missed.

But this was not my only disappointment. In the new elections, Golda Meir's government came into power, and Bentov retired. These events had important repercussions for the Habitat project.

Meir's new Minister of Housing, Zeev Sharef, proceeded vigorously with the strategy of creating an Israeli presence in areas previously controlled by Jordan and now annexed to the new

Jerusalem city limits, in such a way that the north-south border that divided the city between 1948 and 1967 could never be re-established. This was implemented by a series of neighborhoods encircling the city: Ramot Eshkol, French Hill, Ramot Neve Yaakov to the north, and Gilo and East Talpiot to the south (in the annexed sectors of the city). Each would vary in population from ten to fifty thousand. When fully developed all of these neighbourhoods were to house close to a quarter of a million people.

These new neighbourhoods were created in the spirit of an old tradition known as *homa ve migdal* — stockade and tower. Ottoman law held that once a building was constructed and roofed, even if it had been built illegally, the authorities could not demolish it. Through the years preceding the establishment of the state, the pioneer settlers would venture out at night with building materials and rapidly put up a tower with a wall around it, thereby creating the nucleus of a settlement which the authorities could not then demolish. This policy proved successful; a settled region become a living fact.

When the United Nations in 1947 came to divide the country and draw up boundaries, they could not ignore the existence of the settlements. So under the United Nations resolution of 1947, certain parts of the coastal zone and the Negev were given to Israel because they were, in fact, settled. Even areas not originally designated (such as parts of the Galilee) became part of Israel after the 1948 War because Jews settled them, stayed, and defended them through the fighting, and were still there at the time of the signing of the armistice agreement. Thus the act of building had become an expression of the will to remain permanently on the land.

This policy led the government to make many completely illogical city planning decisions. These satellite towns, located for reasons of strategy alone, found themselves cut off without proper services or even road connections. They were built as dormitories and no thought was given to the employment of their residents, who now had to commute by bus and car through several kilometres of wilderness to get to their work in the city proper. At least American suburbs that evolve at the periphery have organic connections to the mother city. In Israel, these artificial satellites were like fetuses with weak umbilical cords.

Habitat '67 — The port of Montreal and the city in the background. *(Graetz Photography)*

Habitat '67 — 20 years later. The roof gardens are lush with vegetation. Trees have grown on the river's edge and life is active in the houses, streets and piazzas.

The ancient village of Manchat — Dilapidated and housing immigrants since 1948, the village would be restored and reconstructed.

Habitat Jerusalem — Close up. Note the prefabricated boxes, the convertible domed gardens, the pedestrian bridgeways clustered on the steep topography.   *(Arnott Rogers Batten Ltd.)*

Hosh — The ruins of Hosh before restoration. *(Yaacov Harlap)*

Hosh — The ancient Hosh Synagogue before restoration. *(Yaacov Harlap)*

Hosh — The restored Hosh with its courtyards, apartments, synagogue. *(David Harris)*

Yeshivat Porat Yosef — The original structure before 1948.

Yeshivat Porat Yosef — The Yeshiva being blown up by the Jordanian Arab Legion, May 1948.

Yeshivat Porat Yosef — The site and ruins of Yeshivat Porat Yosef with the sign announcing the intention to rebuild, 1967. *(Chava Mordochovitch Private Collection)*

Yeshivat Porat Yosef — Detail of the concrete arches and traditional stone vaults.
(Lee English Photos)

Yeshivat Porat Yosef. *(Lee English Photos)*
(Lee English Photos)

Jerusalem — View from Mount Scopus. The Yeshiva is to the left of the dome.

Aerial view of the old city: the Western Wall is in the center and the Yeshiva site to right bottom.

The ruin of Safdie house. This area was to become the central courtyard.

Moshe Safdie during military service in 1972 (center).

The courtyard covered with its glass vaults as an interior garden. Safdie residence.   *(Joan Almond)*

The convertible
glazed dome — interior —
with view
of the Temple Mount.
Safdie residence.
(Joan Almond)

Nevertheless massive resources were directed towards establishing these satellite towns in the newly occupied territories. But Manchat, where I wanted to build the new Habitat, was within the old border and was already a predominantly Jewish district. The project had also been Bentov's baby and with his retirement, the driving force behind the development of Habitat Jerusalem was gone. So my first venture in Israel crashed before it could ever get off the ground.

MAYOR TEDDY KOLLEK

So much of what Jerusalem has become — and what it has avoided — it owes to Teddy Kollek. He has been the principal moving force in the development of Jerusalem since he was elected in 1965, and the city had the good fortune to have him in office during the critical days of reunification in 1967. Those were the days when vital decisions were being made and attitudes being formed: whether the Arab municipality should continue to operate; whether Arabs should be invited to participate in the city council; where the borders of the enlarged metropolitan city, now annexed to Israel, should be; and what rights and services should be given to the Arab population. These crucial matters established the flavor of the Kollek administration. By and large the Arab population of Jerusalem did not accept Israeli rule; certainly they expressed misgivings about not having their own sovereignty. But Kollek navigated through this sea of antagonism, creating as he went more goodwill than one would have expected possible under the circumstances. His diplomacy had a surprisingly positive effect: In the next municipal election the Arabs supported Kollek overwhelmingly, and thus in part were responsible for his re-election.

His sensibilities are expressed in his policies. For example, the Arabs wanted to put up a monument to their soldiers who died during the Six Day War. Israeli nationalists protested. But Teddy's understanding and will prevailed, and there, outside the walls of the Old City, the monument stands. Dozens of such acts softened the tensions and resulted in more tolerance between Jews and Arabs living together in the city.

Mayor Teddy Kollek is one of those few mayors who are world figures and certainly one of the best known Israeli leaders abroad. Before becoming Mayor, he was actively involved in the founding of the state, with immigration, with arms purchasing. Director of Prime Minister David Ben Gurion's office, he became one of his confidants; he set up the Israel Tourist Bureau, which brought international tourism to Israel on a grand scale; he conceived, organized and raised the funds for the Israel Museum. And then he became Jerusalem's Mayor.

As I write this, he has just turned 77. His age has not affected his energy. More youthful than men ten or twenty years younger, he puts in sixteen hours a day. He is of Viennese origin, one of the most cultured and sophisticated men in public life in Israel. His friends include world leaders in the arts, politics and business, people like Isaac Stern, Zubin Mehta, Leonard Bernstein, the Rockefellers, William Paley, the Rothschilds. While he is obviously an Israeli mayor, elected by the residents of his city, his connections are international.

If one tries to imagine someone else in the job, then it becomes immediately clear how fortunate Jerusalem is to have this man — in the eyes of the world he is a trustee of a world treasure and his constituency is international. Through the Jerusalem Foundation (the vehicle of fund-raising abroad) he has brought almost as much money into the city as the taxpayers have raised internally. Similarly Teddy's standing within the city is extranational; he is perceived by the Arab residents as someone they can not only trust but also identify with. This would be out of the question with almost any other Jewish leader including Peres or Rabin.

CHAPTER 3

THE YESHIVA AT THE WALL

When I came back to Israel in 1967, one of the first things I did was to visit Jerusalem. The Six Day War had united the city, divided between Jordan and Israel since 1948, and I made straight for the Western Wall, that remnant of the Second Temple which has such significance for all Judaism. I remembered it from my childhood as a narrow elongated space crammed between buildings, open to the sky, and usually jam-packed with praying Jews.

I was in for a surprise. Immediately after the war, the bulldozers had moved in and opened up a huge area in front of the Wall right across to the edge of the Jewish Quarter, historically known as the Upper City. I stood silently, looking about. There to the east was the great Western Wall of Herod's Temple, which once contained the Ark of the Covenant. To the west was the cliff upon which sits the Jewish Quarter. A line of run-down buildings ran along it, ending at the ruins of a rabbinical college, the Yeshivat Porat Yosef.

For eighty years, this college, or yeshiva, had been an important Jerusalem institution. Gifts from Sephardic Jews in India at the turn of the century had provided for the purchase of the site, and it is still run by, and educates, Sephardic Jews. The first benefactor was Yosef Shalom (its name Porat Yosef commemorates him).

The first yeshiva, a symmetrical building of two wings flanking a central domed structure, was blown up by the Arab Legion in 1948. Now, in 1967, the bulldozers had cleared out the houses that had once separated the yeshiva from the Wall. Thus, the site of the Yeshivat Porat Yosef gained an importance it had never before enjoyed.

I noticed a new sign on the destroyed college:

"Here on its original site, as a symbol of our return to Old Jerusalem, will be rebuilt the Yeshivat Porat Yosef, a building destroyed in 1948."

Something clicked inside me — I had a curious feeling that all of my life had been leading up to this. The Western Wall . . . the Old City . . . the site overlooking the Holy of Holies . . . a Sephardic rabbinical college. As much as I wanted the task of designing this Sephardic institution in the heart of Jerusalem, I had to blink the dream away. I had discovered after a few inquiries that the building had already been commissioned to Israeli architects.

Being Sephardic, I did have family connections with the yeshiva: my uncle Joseph Shamah was a member of the congregation and had been actively involved with its administration; his daughter was married to one of the two rabbis in charge; their legal counsel and trustee was also a distant cousin. All, including me, were Jews with origins in Aleppo, Syria, making us in a sense part of a greater expanded family (for every Aleppo Jew assumes that every other Jew from Aleppo is a blood relative in one way or another).

Despite these rabbinical family connections with my uncle Joseph Shamah and my cousin's husband, I did not really feel part of the very religious Orthodox side of the family. My parents had brought me up in Haifa in a secular, though traditional, environment.

There is an enormous difference between the lifestyle of secular and Orthodox Jews in Israel, and this difference is reflected geographically as well. Haifa was nicknamed the Red City, the socialist city, because it was a city of industry, of labor unions, and of many intellectuals of German origin. Having arrived at the beginning of the Nazi persecution, Jewish immigrants in Haifa had continued their secular European lifestyle and therefore carried completely different cultural overtones than, say, those religious Jews from the shtetls (homesteads) of Eastern Europe. For example, to this day, Haifa's bus system runs regularly on Saturday, whereas the religious political lobby has succeeded in halting this convenience in every other city in Israel.

Being a secular family, on Saturdays we would pack picnics and take a taxi or a bus to the Mediterranean beaches, or in spring to the mountains, where we'd make a campfire. In 1947, we bought a car (the first Studebaker to arrive in Israel) and we were able to drive to Nazareth to visit the traditional Arab garden restaurants for their stuffed vegetables, pigeons, and other wonderful delicacies. Our weekends were full of excitement, whereas a religious family, forbidden to drive, would walk to synagogue where they spent most of the day or else they would remain quietly at home.

We did not keep a kosher house, meaning my parents didn't separate milk and meat dishes with two sets of cutlery and two sinks.

During the Second World War when I was very young, Haifa was bombed by the Italians, so the whole family went to live with our Orthodox relatives Aunt Gladys and Uncle Joseph, who lived in Jerusalem. My brother Gabriel was born there. Later, I was often sent to Jerusalem for holidays, or for a whole month in summer. These visits were a cultural shock. No light could be switched on after the sun set on Friday. Dietary practice was of great importance. Once I'd eaten meat I had to wait six hours before I could drink milk, and if I drank it earlier I was sinning. They took it all with such fervent passion.

An added element was their zeal to reform us: we had obviously gone astray and our brief stays in Jerusalem provided an ideal opportunity for them to bring us back into the fold. So when they went to synagogue to pray, three times every weekday, they insisted that I go with them. I was young, easily intimidated, and I went. And of course I could do almost nothing on Saturday.

Still, I had my limits. I remember vividly being offered one pound sterling (then worth $5, a lot of money!) if I promised not to turn on an electric switch on the Sabbath for a period of one year. Already I proved to be a bad businessman by refusing on principle.

It was some months after I first saw the sign on the yeshiva that events took me back to Israel. Among a long list of things to do was a note from my parents: "Remember to call cousin Yaffa and give her our regards." As I mentioned, Yaffa was married to the rabbi of the yeshiva, Moshe Shrem.

I phoned cousin Yaffa, passed on the regards and asked, "How are things?"

"Well, things are really not very good," she replied. "They've had a great deal of trouble with the design of the yeshiva. No one liked the plans those Israeli architects made."

The Israelis had been dismissed and an American architect had been brought in, she went on. He had proposed a great cube completely enclosed in stained glass, which the planning authorities felt to be totally inappropriate. So now they had two sets of plans behind them and were going nowhere. Everybody was very upset, because the government was trying to get the Jewish Quarter reconstructed as quickly as possible and the pressure to build in Jerusalem was enormous.

Just before hanging up, she said, "You wouldn't be interested, would you?"

I laughed and mumbled, "I might, I might."

Half an hour later, a phone call came, and a meeting was set up for that afternoon in the lobby of the Basel Hotel in Tel Aviv with the two rabbis. It was February 1970.

As I waited for them, I reflected on my strong emotional interest in the project: I understood the architecture of the Middle East as well as anybody, perhaps better; I grew up in Israel, spent much of my life in Jerusalem. I was not an import, I was native. But I was nonetheless apprehensive.

The two rabbis, Moshe and Avraham Shrem, walked in, accompanied by a third person, Stephen Shalom. Rabbi Avraham Shrem was broad, on the plump side, round-faced, beardless then, wearing, as always, a dark suit and black rimmed glasses, very emotional and fast-talking. His brother Moshe was thin, slight, a small man with a thin black beard and dark eyebrows, nervous and intense.

Stephen Shalom's father had been one of the main benefactors of the first Yeshivat Porat Yosef, though curiously enough he was not related to the Yosef Shalom, the benefactor whom it commemorated. Known as "the handkerchief king of New York," Stephen's father was an Aleppo Jew who went to the United States and became a successful importer of dry goods. His three sons went into banking, shipping, and real estate development.

Stephen, with his knowledge of real estate, had been on the building committees of hospitals and schools in New York. He was in his mid-forties but looked much younger, with blue eyes, slightly curly hair, and a rather round face. He was a cultured, second-generation New York businessman and philanthropist. He was a major fund-raiser for Israeli bonds and the United Jewish Appeal and a member of several of the Israeli Prime Minister's advisory committees. Not religious in his daily life, he has often claimed to be most likely to give financial support to a technical school, hospital or clinic. But his father had made a lifelong commitment to the yeshiva (and is buried on the Mount of Olives, which overlooks the yeshiva); thus Stephen felt it was proper to donate to the reconstruction.

We talked about the site and the program. Then Rabbi Avraham Shrem asked: "Will you design for us a traditional building or a modern building?"

It was a tough question on two counts. First, there was the real issue of the relationship of this new building to the architectural heritage surrounding the site. The yeshiva itself had been demolished, but it was now surrounded by ancient buildings, some Ottoman, others from even earlier periods. As always the question was this: How does one relate the new to the old — to the Wall, the mosques and domes, the arches, cliffs, courtyards — to everything that makes the architecture of Old Jerusalem?

Second, two architects had already been fired: one for a modern building that did not harmonize; the other for a massive building that the rabbis and Stephen felt was eclectic, i.e., that mimicked the shapes and forms of the surroundings in a simplistic manner. So how should I answer that question — being interviewed as I was for a job I very much wanted?

I had a strong feeling that it must be a building that looked as if it had always been there. At the same time I didn't want it to be lost in the urban fabric — I wanted it to have its own identity. I wanted it to be clearly an expression of today, yet with a quality of timelessness. Of course, I hadn't even begun to design it, so my answer had to be intuitive. I paused, and then found myself saying, "If I succeed, you won't be able to answer this question." They seemed pleased. But having been burned twice, they told me they could not make another firm commitment. Would I first do a conceptual design? If they approved it, they would then commission me to design the building. This conceptual phase I estimated would cost thirty or forty thousand dollars; of course, they wanted it done for nothing. After some horse-trading, we settled on ten thousand dollars. I was to present a plan in three months.

I spent the next two or three days getting site information. I talked to the people at the Company for the Reconstruction and Development of the Jewish Quarter. This organization had been set up in 1967 to reconstruct and repopulate the Quarter after it was partially destroyed by Jordan's Arab Legion in 1948.

I uncovered some strange problems. Apparently the general site area on which the old yeshiva stood had been designated by the government for the construction of two new yeshivas: Porat Yosef, which was Sephardic, and Yeshivat Hakotel, which was Ashkenazi. Already the two institutions and their architects had started fighting, first about the definition of the sites, and second about the height, each side trying to outdo the other. Matters had become so unpleasant that a Cabinet committee was forced to arbitrate. By the time I came on the scene, problems between the two yeshivas had been resolved. Strict height and volume restrictions were imposed on both sides. So I had to contend not only with the issues of the old and the new, but also with height and width restrictions. To complicate the design even more, I had to take into account the yeshiva next door which had not itself been designed.

I flew back to Montreal. Generally, I work quite fast once I have a new commission. Having visited the site with the client and absorbed the program, I would develop the first ideas on the flight back home. But this flight was different. I was paralyzed. At the end of the trip my sketchbook was almost empty. And the paralysis went on for several weeks.

Another major restriction was that Old City by-laws required all buildings to be built of the gold-yellow Jerusalem limestone. The yeshiva was in the Jewish Quarter, which had even sricter by-laws: roofs and terraces had to be paved with that particular stone. That meant one should use stone not as a veneer, but in the traditional way as the principal load bearing material.

Louis Kahn (the architect for whom I apprenticed) religiously respected the nature of materials and described brick, stone, or concrete as each having its own specific "character." I too was inclined not to use stone as just a veneer. On the other hand, this was not the time of Hadrian or Byzantium and here was I, fresh from Habitat, convinced, perhaps a little naively, of the virtues of prefabrication and building industrialization.

We build with the technology of our time. One of the great joys one derives from experiencing a work of architecture is to understand how it was built, how it stands up: stone bearing on stone, brick on brick, the awareness of how the ceiling is held up by beams and joists, or small stones forming a vault. Architectural style must be linked to the methodology of building and to the available materials being used, as can be seen in the different styles of periods and places. One of my pet irritations is the misconception that style is a formal, visual language, independent of technique, to be applied in a free-wheeling way to the envelope of a building.

An architect often faces the layman's question "What is the style of your architecture?" or the more difficult question posed by clients "In what style will you make this building?" The question is rooted in the popular conception that architectural design emerges from two independent sets of concern. First, you fulfill the requirements of the program of space required and satisfy the technical requirements so that the building stands up, is properly heated, ventilated and water-proofed. Then you apply the trimmings to the utilitarian package you have conceived and make it Tudor, Gothic, Spanish, art deco, or modern. In this view style comes out of a pattern book, an inventory of elements: arches, white stucco and red tiles yield Spanish; porticos, colonnades and pediments yield classical; mixing these features with brick walls yields Georgian. This traditional attitude toward style is echoed in contemporary attitudes toward design. Critics speak of the architect as having chosen to make a building in a particular style.

Everything about my education and upbringing defies this dualism, or artificial separation. Planning, creating space and structures, craftsmanship and construction, even creating ornament and decoration, are a single integrated and interdependent process of synthesis. Those who evolved the Gothic style were not partaking in an exercise of mimicry but exploring stone construction and aspiring to create space with spiritual and religious feelings. Peasants in Nubia or New Mexico using mud brick and adobe with brick vaults or thatched roofs were similarly evolving style as the expression of process. Nowhere has the question of appropriate style and its connection with process been more alive than in designing in the Old City of Jerusalem.

Should I build a structure that would essentially be a reproduction of the ancient structures in the Old City? I would have felt uncomfortable about doing in 1969 what was appropriate to 1869 or 1669. The construction industry in Jerusalem was geared to mass-construction building techniques and to contemporary construction materials — getting good stonemasons would not be easy. It was therefore clear to me that building in the traditional way would also take a lot of money. (One senses the anachronism of this approach when visiting the Holy Sepulchre, where old masons were laboriously remaking capitals, columns and cornices for the church's restoration.)

The issue of the spatial requirements of the yeshiva also concerned me. In Habitat, the building system consisted of identical room-size elements that could be combined in different ways to make up maybe a dozen different apartment types. But here, the synagogue could be twenty metres square and five storeys high, a dormitory room might be three by five metres, a dining room twenty by thirty. Could a single building element create this variety of spaces?

Today, an infinite variety of modes of construction are mixed together in every building: long steel trusses for roofs (hidden by suspended acoustic tiles), concrete walls covered by a thin stone veneer, roofs made of concrete, steel or wood — each material manipulated to form an endless parade of shapes, totally independent of the character and nature of the materials themselves.

In Habitat I was searching for a method by which a single construction element ("a giant brick" the size of one or two rooms) would suffice. This time my search, which became an obsession, was for another contemporary equivalent of the brick, an element much larger in scale, fabricated by machine, something lifted with a crane rather than by hand, which could then be assembled to form large and small spaces, from small dormitory rooms to a great synagogue. Something comparable in concept to a brick on a giant scale.

A little brick, eight by four inches, can form both small and big rooms. When used without steel or wood or concrete beams, the brick is used to make walls, and alone it can form the ceilings but then they must be vaults. Or think of the Gothic cathedral: its spires, flying buttresses, vaults and nave chapels are all variations on a singular methodology governed by its own intrinsic order and logic.

I wanted to rediscover that sense of unity and integrity that I sensed in medieval buildings. I was convinced that if I limited the palate of building components I might find an element that would result in a formal language as compelling as that of brick buildings.

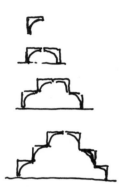

So there I was, endlessly sketching, while preliminary work continued in my office in Montreal. A model had been made of the site showing the surrounding buildings and the contours, and wood blocks had been cut to represent the volumes of the various rooms and the synagogue. I was exploring different possible arrangements to fit all these little coloured wood blocks on the site — when all of a sudden it hit me. Why not make the rooms of large prefabricated arches?

If we had a standard arch three metres high, a half-arch could be used to form both large and small rooms. Two half-arches would connect to make one arch six metres wide — forming a room six metres square. The arch form could be further combined by pyramiding arches one upon the other, making a tracery of arched elements for the taller rooms. But all the while, regardless of room size, the combination of the three-metre element would preserve the basic small scale as well as evoking the scale and forms of the ancient surrounding buildings.

What about the questions of whether to use stone or concrete, old or new, traditional or contemporary construction? Often, the simplest solutions are the hardest to find. I decided to use real stone construction selectively for the walls that defined the boundaries of the site and the main sections then within these compounds to use prefabricated concrete for the single standardized element which was the half-arch.

As this central concept became clear, we began building a presentation model, and the pace changed in the office. At the same time, we resorted to a rather unorthodox approach. Models usually are assembled from cardboard or wood after the drawings have been made, each piece being cut by hand to its specific dimensions. But here the idea of a single building element forced us to reverse the process: we first stamped out hundreds of cardboard pieces to represent the identical three metre arches. To represent the stone walls, we used cork, cut in slabs approximately one inch thick.

Since each room in the building was to be constructed out of these two elements, I began the process of designing with the models first. We soon realized from their complexity that our results could never have been achieved through two-dimensional designs alone. Each part of the building was assembled, examined, changed and adapted. Once satisfied, we proceeded to draw it up; hence, the model workshop became the center for the development of the design.

When a room was formed by the arches, it could be extended outwards in the shape of a transparent domed window. The dome-shaped windows, all of different sizes, gave us problems. How were we going to make them for the model? We searched the toy shops for transparent balls, but found nothing suitable. Then our model maker, Raoul, remembered seeing a vacuum-forming machine used for making toy cars. He suggested we make our own machine. We tried building a dome out of wood, making little holes so that air could be sucked through. Then we hooked the contraption onto a vacuum cleaner, used a hot plate to soften plastic sheeting — and lo and behold, it worked! Our own vacuum-forming machine could make domes of any shape to fit the model. At once this rather crude mock-up of cork and cardboard became a most sophisticated presentation model, all due to the wonderful bubbles of clear plastic we were able to make.

During the last week leading to the presentation of the design the whole office went on a charette, pulling drawings together, completing the model and renderings. By then we knew exactly what we were after — all we had to do was find the best way to show it to the client. Every few hours we came together, discussed what we had done, made certain decisions, broke for dinner, returned, stayed late, worked, ate, worked, slept, on and on, until at last, there it was — a large model of the complete building with a series of sketches and plans that represented it on paper.

At long last, it was time to go to Jerusalem and make the presentation. For three months we had been working wihout contact with the client, an unusual situation for an architect. The client is usually in the same city. He sees the design as it evolves, and by the time the moment of presentation arrives, he has become part and parcel of the process. Not so in this case. We worried how the rabbis and Stephen Shalom would react. Would they like the design? And even if they did, how would the municipal authorities receive it? Would they approve concrete arches when the building ordinances specifically restricted any material but stone? With a lot of enthusiasm, but also a good deal of anxiety, I began preparing for the trip to Jerusalem.

THE ARCHITECTURAL PROCESS

The process of designing a building in an architectural office can be visualized as an ever-expanding cone, drawing in more and more people from the first moment of encounter with the client, the project and the site to the completion of construction. Designing a house is obviously very different from designing a museum or library. One researches the program and building type; one might visit other museums or libraries, as the case may be. Often one is presented with a detailed program of requirements which might include elaborate technical needs to be fulfilled.

The shape and orientation of the site, the surrounding context (be it urban or rural), the connection between site and surrounding buildings are all factors to be considered in the design. In fact the site not only situates the building but should generate the design ideas.

The first step, at the tip of the cone, is the lonely process of exploration. It might take the form of small ink doodles in a sketchbook, tiny diagrams of the organization of a building and its basic shapes. It might take a three-dimensional form in little models of clay or wood, clumsily assembled to explore embryonic ideas.

Soon there emerges a "parti." Sometimes there might be two or three alternatives. Then come the diagrams which suggest a juxtaposition of parts. The expanding cone then draws in more individuals. A large model is constructed of the site and the surrounding buildings. Floors, walls, rooms are built into it, pushed about, as others in the office begin drawing plans and sections to scale, fitting things more carefully to the context of the site. Others begin important technical explorations: what are the relevant building codes, zoning parameters, materials and methods appropriate to this project? Specialists are called in: what are the requirements for the kitchens and food services, acoustics; what are the likely energy sources, heating and cooling methods? Design then arrives at a presentation phase — drawings and models become legible and one can explain the idea of the building to the client.

Explaining the building in itself is always a challenge. Drawings and sketches meaningful to the architect may mean little to the layman. Much larger models, realistic in their rendition of materials, as well as perspectives and montages, are made, which then bring the building to life in clear three-dimensional form.

With the approval of the client, the cone further expands into a more specialized phase as the drawings are prepared. At this point, the building is dissected and separated into many different parts. A building such as Yeshivat Porat Yosef involves at least ten architects with almost an equal number of engineers and other consultants. Some are drawing sections through walls or designing windows and ceilings while others are busy detailing the finishing touches — material selections or the specifications which involve the choosing of everything from door knobs and light switches to the basic surfaces and materials of the building. For a small building this might take three or four months; for a large building a year or more. A house might involve twenty drawings and an institution two hundred or more. Computers are useful both in making drawings and in coordination.

Finally, we produce the construction document set of drawings, which are turned over to the contractors, the craftsmen and the workmen, and the construction begins.

CHAPTER 4

AT WORK ON THE YESHIVA

By now I was experienced in taking models through customs. At one time, we would arrive at airports around the world with these big wooden crates, all bolted up, and invariably the customs officials would insist on undoing all the bolts and looking inside. So we devised our own time-saver — windows. The officials could then inspect the crates by looking through these windows. We found too that even the baggage handlers treat crates containing windows with the utmost respect. On the other hand, a window invites free reviews.

At Montreal airport where we cleared Canadian customs, I received a critique on the merits of Middle Eastern architecture. Peering through the window of the case, the good natured Canadian customs official summarily pronounced the model of the yeshiva to look like a sheik's palace and concluded that its destination was Arabia. Close to Arabia, I pointed out — across the border in Israel.

The scene at Lod Airport was rather a contrast. There the customs officials' primary interest is in discovering illegally imported electrical appliances, especially televisions and stereos. Our crate was large enough to arouse exuberant fantasies of an enormous catch.

The junior official summoned the next in line, and he got hold of his superior. They crowded around the case, all peering in with the aid of a flashlight. When they finally saw what it really was, I was waved through.

Outside, three colleagues from my new office were waiting with a half-ton truck to take the model to Jerusalem. The presentation was to be made in the Old City where motor vehicles are not permitted, so we had to park the truck several hundred yards away and carry the case, like some kind of coffin, across the open space in front of the Western Wall, right into the yeshiva's temporary offices.

In the plain room exposed fluorescent tubes threw a bluish light. The rabbis and their building committee, mostly bearded and dressed in black, were waiting on folding chairs around a makeshift table. Stephen Shalom, the major benefactor in the project, was wearing a colorful cotton shirt and sports slacks. We all wore skullcaps out of respect.

It took us some moments to get the crate unpacked. Then the top came off, we lifted the model out of the crate, and I thought I heard a sigh of disbelief as we placed it on the table. For a moment everybody was silent.

Perhaps they had expected a massive block model devoid of detail or perhaps they had simply expected a familiar building — walls rising with punched windows and some special element marking the synagogue. But as the cover was removed, even under the flat fluorescent lights, the model came to life — animated and vibrant, the tracery of arches forming complex shadows, the eye leading through the glazed openings to glimpses of the interior of the synagogue and the dining room. They rose to their feet and leaned over the model peeking in with an air of children exploring a new toy. At first they seemed hesitant, as if afraid that it might bite, but then their confidence increased as they grasped the visual richness and complexity. While it was unlike any other building they had seen, the unfamiliar forms did not seem to shock them. What was wonderful about that first unveiling was that it prompted everyone to break into a smile. Shalom loved the model, the rabbis loved it, the building committee loved it. Then they all became excited. The model was an instant success.

The design had some controversial features, however. I wanted to create a duet between the massiveness of the stone walls and the lightness of the concrete arches. I decided to pierce the massive exterior walls with vertical slots so that from outside, one got a hint of the lace-like arched structure behind. From inside, one would look out through large arched windows into a stone cove formed by the curved outer wall; light from the sky and sun would then be reflected into the room, reducing the glare and making a splendid contrast between the sun-flooded city and darker interior spaces. At the centre of each curve, the walls would part to make vertical slots through which glimpses of the city could be seen, giving a gradual transition from the window, through the walled exterior space, and on out towards the ancient buildings and Western Wall.

In Jerusalem, the buildings of institutions were always understated; their guts were never exposed to the public, just glimpses and hints. I'll never forget my first visit to the Holy Sepulchre: we walked up a narrow alley, no more than eight feet wide, to an ordinary door with a small cross carved in stone above. Passing through the door we found ourselves in the large courtyard of the Holy Sepulchre,

looking at the two great entrance arches and the three domes. That sudden, shocking transformation of walking through that door and passing from the tight scale of the alley into the grand institution was an experience that always stayed with me. The same transformation takes place as you enter the Temple Mount through the small wooden doors from the narrow alleyways. There, suddenly, are acres of terraced expanse, with the great golden Dome of the Rock and the ancient al-Aksa Mosque.

That was what I wanted with the yeshiva. From the Western Wall, one should get glimpses, but it would be wrong to reveal the entire yeshiva at once. The stone wall should be a screen with a sense of mystery, behind which unknown things happened. Then, as one entered the small main gate, the study hall, the courtyards, the synagogue, one space after another, would gradually be revealed.

Models of the dining room, of a typical dorm, classroom, a large model of the synagogue, and of the study hall were presented to Stephen and to the rabbis at lengthy meetings. By and large it was a very smooth process, though on occasion there was some discord.

At one of the meetings, Rabbi Avraham Shrem asked for the synagogue to be raised so as to get a better view of the Western Wall through the window behind the Ark. I had studied the sitelines carefully to make sure the people praying at the Wall would be clearly visible from the seats on the main floor of the synagogue. I knew that if it was raised, one would see less. But as I was to discover later, Rabbi Shrem always disguised his true objective. In this case, what he really wanted was to make the whole mass of the synagogue higher so that it would eclipse the Ashkenazi rabbinical college behind us. I argued that the massing was carefully placed and it

would be wrong to make the synagogue any higher. Anything larger than the six storey mass would be totally out of scale with the surroundings.

For my part I wondered: why not integrate the synagogue with the study hall, since the study hall (Beit Midrash) is, in reality, itself a synagogue? Rabbis-to-be do not learn in a typical classroom setting; rather they sit in groups of two and three around little tables and at the top of their voices practice and discuss the interpretation of the scriptures and the Talmud, while their teachers, themselves rabbis, move from table to table giving guidance.

I was told that combining the synagogue and study hall would create too much conflict between the public and private domain. People coming to pray on high holidays and the Sabbath, as well as the constant stream of pilgrims, would distract the students from their studies. Two great halls, they believed, were necessary.

The study hall, where the young men, two or three hundred of them, would spend many hours a day, I imagined as a bright room, open in all directions, with views and with breezes blowing through it. It must have ample natural light for reading (all that small print), so that no artificial light would be necessary during the day.

The synagogue was another matter. Its function did not allow a simple programmatic definition. What is a synagogue? It's not a church or a mosque, for Jewish ritual makes it more a community meeting house. Any ten adult Jewish males praying anywhere constitutes a minyan, a quorum. A synagogue is a place for speaking to God on your own, and at the same time speaking to Him in community.

There are two principal elements to the synagogue: the Ark (Aron Kodesh) and the bimah. The Ark is where the scriptures are kept and it is always located in the direction of Jerusalem and the Temple Mount. The bimah from which the Scriptures are read is in the center of the room. The Sephardic synagogue, unlike the Ashkenazic synagogue, is not set up with the seats of the congregation facing the Ark but with the seating in the round focusing on the bimah. This arrangement emphasizes a sense of community and establishes the principal of direct communication with God without intermediaries. Liturgically, it seemed completely right to have the synagogue bathed with soft light coming down through the skylights and a translucent roof above.

Central to my thinking about the design of the synagogue was that it was to be the principal Sephardic synagogue in Israel, perhaps in the world. People would come from all over the world to pray there, as they come to Jerusalem and to the Wall. The Western Wall and, rising above it, the Temple Mount should be part of the experience of praying in the synagogue. So I organized the room on a single axis on which the bimah, the Ark and the Western Wall and the site of the Temple stood in one line, bringing the Temple Mount and the Wall visually into the synagogue.

As it evolved, the duet I was developing between stone and concrete arches created in the synagogue the effect of a room within a room. Massive stone walls formed the outer shell, but inside, the lacey structure of the pyramiding arches formed an inner container and so, unlike most rooms, the synagogue had no precise envelope but layers of depth, something like a view of cliff-like hills through a foreground of trees. Light would come washing down from the skylights and over the stone walls, which parted along the axis to reveal the view of the Temple Mount.

In one of our meetings, a rabbi asked, "How about stained glass?"

I confess I was a bit indignant because I felt stained glass had no place in a synagogue. Gothic churches had given me the most wonderful experiences through their stained glass, their colours, their stories told through images. But Judaism forbids the making of images.

"How could we possibly use stained glass?" I retorted. "You shall not make for yourself a graven image or any likeness of anything . . ."

"Don't worry," said the rabbi, "just make it an abstract design."

I continued to resist, believing him influenced by the abandoned design proposed by the American architect, a huge cube surrounded with stained glass. But behind his request, I could sense a desire for the festivity of colour.

One day back in Montreal, I was thinking, skylights . . . sun . . . Jerusalem . . . colour — and then like a thunderbolt, it came to me: prisms.

I rushed down to a hobby shop on Ste. Catherine Street, bought a lot of one inch wide prisms, hurried back to the office, and took the model of the synagogue up to the roof. There I placed the prisms in the model above the skylights. Montreal is not Jerusalem but it was a sunny day and the sun burst into the model through the prisms, covering the walls with the whole spectrum of colours.

Coloured light could flood the space, just like stained glass. I turned the model, imitating the movement of the sun. The patterns of colours on the walls changed too. Broad strokes of the spectrum became beams of light, bands of blues and reds and purples in endless variety. I called Stephen Shalom to tell him what I'd done, then rushed to New York to share it with him.

There was, however, a serious question to be answered: Would it work life size? A one inch prism on the scale of the model meant a three or four feet wide prism in the real yeshiva. I remembered reading about a New York artist, Charles Ross, who had been experimenting with prisms — so I called him and arranged a meeting.

I found he had developed a number of prisms of quite substantial size, building them out of acrylic and filling them with mineral oil, adding a tank to allow the expansion and contraction of the liquid as the prisms heated and cooled.

We built a much larger model, four or five feet square, and Charles started to experiment with the placement of prisms in the model. We still weren't sure the prisms would work at life size. My conversations with opticists at McGill University left things nervously inconclusive. So I went back to Stephen and said that there was only one way to be sure — build a life-size mock-up.

On a parking lot that Stephen Shalom owns in Queens, we constructed a full-size canvas mock-up of one of the semi-circular stone shafts that form the walls of the synagogue. Charles Ross made three prisms, each fifteen feet long, filled with mineral oil. A little crane hoisted them up into location. We waited for the sun to break from behind a bank of clouds. Suddenly, it found an opening. We stared in awe as all the brilliant colours of the spectrum came flooding down the canvas wall . . . .

Notwithstanding the enthusiasm these designs were creating in Israel, we all knew that the process of getting approval for plans in Jerusalem was very complex and until the municipality and the District Commission approved the plan, we couldn't build. So after that first presentation of my designs, I decided to revise the model and the drawings right away and submit them to the authorities.

I was soon back in Jerusalem with a more elaborate model and drawings, which I presented to the Municipal Planning Council. They immediately objected that the arches made of concrete were visible from the outside. While the site itself was defined by massive stone walls, they pointed out that above them the lacework of the concrete arches could be seen, in contradiction of the by-law that stated "stone only."

I explained that we proposed to use Jerusalem limestone as the aggregate for the concrete and that sandblasting the concrete after it was poured would expose the golden stone on the surface, making it the colour of the stone walls. This explanation was satisfactory and the plan was approved by the Council. Soon after, with haste I've never again experienced in Jerusalem, I was asked to present the plans to the District Commission. Again, great enthusiasm. With a couple of cautionary provisos, the plan received their blessing too.

Drafting the contract for architectural services began during that honeymoon with the rabbis. For reasons I can't explain, I gave the contract more attention than I usually do. It turned out to be time well spent.

I took the standard contract of the American Institute of Architects and translated it into Hebrew. But as I worked through it, many questions emerged. Based as I was in Montreal, I might not be on site at all times to supervise construction. Once the client had approved the plans, I had to make sure they would not be changed without my written authorization.

Suppose the client also requested changes for programmatic or functional reasons, once the building was under way? I suggested these be incorporated only with my approval. The rabbis' attorney insisted they have the right to ask for functional changes, with my approval to be withheld only if these changes did not meet my best professional judgement.

The rabbis' attorney also proposed a clause stating that the building committee of the yeshiva was a body of laymen who knew nothing about building practices and consequently were turning to me as "an architect of world renown" (their words, not mine). I was to assume full responsibility for the technical and professional decisions that had to be made, thereby absolving the committee from responsibility for any technical problems or errors that might arise in the future. They were saying, "We're laymen, we know nothing about building, we look to you to make the decisions." These added clauses were all to have repercussions later on.

During the process of developing detailed plans with the two rabbis, their building committee, and Stephen Shalom (the client's de facto representative on a day-to-day basis), I came to know them all fairly well — and to become aware of the great difference between their personalities and cultures.

The two rabbis would look over the plans and speak in generalities; Stephen would read the plans carefully and talk in specifics. Rabbi Avraham Shrem would look at the model, point at the massive stone wall of the synagogue, and say, "Don't you think this needs a little bit of decoration?" or "Wouldn't it be nice if we had a candelabra carved into the stone?" Clearly he was troubled by the severity of some of the design.

Stephen, in contrast, would constantly try to get the rabbis to appreciate the building as it would be used and experienced. He would point to the plans, forcing them to walk down corridors, come through doors, questioning whether doors should open in particular ways, whether a certain room should open into others, whether certain functions shouldn't be relocated. He wanted to know how windows got cleaned; how energy-efficient the heating and cooling system would be. He was equally interested in the visual qualities of the building and how it would fit into the Old City.

He raised valid questions about how education in the yeshiva might change. "Should you not have more classrooms?" he would ask. "Shouldn't there be smaller rooms where a teacher and some students could have a seminar? Shouldn't there be a place where the students could exercise physically?" At that point we introduced a gymnasium and a swimming pool, which the rabbis endorsed — for the moment.

Try as I might, I could not get the rabbis to go through the drawings and truly understand the building. At that moment, they were obsessed with fund-raising. Fund-raising meant rooms that could be named and sold. They also seemed to think that anything on paper was still fluid and they would have ample opportunity to change it later.

My relations with Stephen and with the rabbis reminded me of Louis Sullivan's dictum, in his book *Kindergarten Chats*, that no architect can transcend his client; the quality of a building is as good as the quality of the client, and every client gets the architect he deserves. Conversely, every architect gets the client he deserves.

Even as the plans were being approved and duly signed by the rabbis, and the construction bids were coming in (within the seven million dollar budget), I was forever thinking of Sullivan and his statement. When the contract was signed in 1971 and we started the long process of excavating the rock and constructing the foundations, I wondered which of the two very different clients I deserved. Would I be able to transcend the rabbis with their limited, one-sided and ultimately destructive attitudes toward the yeshiva? Would Stephen's view prevail?

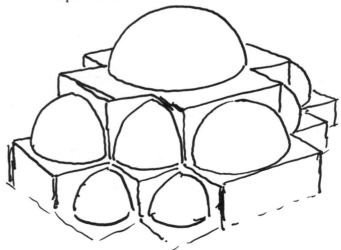

CHAPTER 5

RESTORATIONS OF THE JEWISH QUARTER

During the War of Independence in 1948 the Jewish part of Jerusalem was under siege. The city was cut off from the rest of the Jewish population in the country. Water and food were rationed. It was reminiscent of so many other sieges of Jerusalem — by Titus, Nebuchadnezzar, the Assyrians, the Greeks.

But within this siege was yet another siege: the Jewish Quarter in the walled city was cut off from the rest of the Jewish population of Jerusalem. It was a pitiful situation. In the Quarter were mostly old people, some women and children, and a few fighters — all isolated. Jews outside the Quarter made many attempts to break through the wall and through Zion Gate, but they all failed. As supplies and food ran out, the Jewish Quarter surrendered.

The 1948 war was primitive by modern standards. Rifles, machine guns, and a few mortars were the main weapons. No artillery and certainly no air force bombardment were used in Jerusalem. The physical damage to the Jewish Quarter before the surrender was therefore relatively slight. But then came the great act of destruction: The Arab Legion (the official Jordanian army) moved in and, like the armies of Titus and of Nebuchadnezzar centuries before, systematically destroyed all the monuments, institutions and great synagogues of the Jewish Quarter. This was not done in the heat of battle but by official order. Explosives were placed carefully and thoughtfully under the springing points of the domes, of the great Hurva synagogue, the Nissan Bek synagogue, Yeshivat Porat Yosef, Misgav Ladach Hospital. When it was over the Jewish Quarter lay in ruins.

Shortly after the armistice in 1948, Arab squatters from Hebron, Bethlehem, and other villages moved into the houses that had survived destruction in the Jewish Quarter. By 1967 when the Israelis returned, they found about a third of the buildings had been totally destroyed, a third were very badly damaged, and the rest, through neglect, were in serious disrepair.

The government acted rapidly. It expropriated all land and buildings in the Quarter. This included land and buildings owned by Jews before 1948 as well as by Arabs. Everything from the Western Wall to the edge of the Armenian Quarter became government property. The only exceptions were three Muslim holy places within the Quarter, including two Mameluke buildings, the grave of a sheik, an ancient school that was not in use, and a mosque. These remained in the hands of the Waqf, the Holy Muslim Council which administers all Muslim holy sites.

The government then decided that the entire Quarter would be restored, rebuilt and inhabited by Jews. When it became clear that the task of restoration would be extremely costly and could not be left to private enterprise, it created the Company for the Reconstruction and Development of the Jewish Quarter. Its first task was to clear out and resettle Arabs who were living in the Quarter; its second, to plan the restoration and carry out construction; and its third, to populate the Quarter with Jewish Israelis.

As soon as the Company was created, all buildings and restoration plans became subject to the approval of this group — including, of course, my designs for the Yeshivat Porat Yosef. Accordingly, I made contact with Yehuda Tamir, the Company's chairman. He and his staff endorsed the design and they seemed to appreciate its qualities because they then invited me to design an area of the Jewish Quarter called Block 38. This area was bounded by the Western Wall on the east, by the yeshiva to the south, by the markets to the north, and by Misgav Ladach Street to the west. Block 38 therefore included those buildings that form the edge of the piazza opposite the Western Wall.

Before the contract was signed, Tamir made one condition: I must open an office in Jerusalem and all drawings and designs for Block 38 would be undertaken in Jerusalem under my direction. He felt, as I did, that most of the planning should be done on location, and even the finished plans would need constant modification to meet field conditions.

So in 1970 I made a move of major consequence to my professional and personal life by opening an office in the heart of the Jewish Quarter, and within a few weeks I had hired a number of local architects to join me in developing plans.

Before beginning the design process, I walked as usual through the area. All the houses along the western boundary, Misgav Ladach Street, were in terrible condition but intact. Two of them had large central courtyards open to the sky and a variety of rooms surrounding them — vaulted, domed. Some domes had collapsed from disrepair but I could see the possibility for wonderful apartments, roof terraces, gardens and communal courtyards. Then as we moved beyond the first row of buildings defining the street towards the Western Wall I found great gaps, collapsed buildings, exploded cisterns. Here I would have to build anew, weaving new buildings between the remaining buildings, making a new tapestry of the old and the new. There would, be, therefore, two processes: restoring the old buildings and constructing brand new ones. This was to prove to be a very different experience; on the one hand learning from what was there and on the other applying to the new what was learned from the old.

Walking along I came across a ruin directly overlooking the Western Wall. I found that this was slated for self-restoration (the Company had adopted the policy that larger and more complicated structures could be leased directly to individuals who would see to the restoration themselves and thus minimize the public subsidies) but so far there had been no takers. It was in particularly bad condition and almost adjacent to the Arab market. I loved it and immediately applied to the Company for the 99 year lease offered for self-restoration.

I now had a decidedly personal involvement in the whole project, and in fact my house posed many of the problems that the restorations as a whole did. A single room at street level remained from what was probably a Crusader residence. The second, and main, floor sat in part over the Crusader house and its Ottoman addition. Two of the rooms had damaged but very beautiful domes, one forming a bridge over Misgav Ladach Street. A third room overlooked the Wall. In the middle of these three rooms was an open courtyard. It was hard to tell if the rooms had been built by Jews or Arabs: there were no distinguishing characteristics between domestic Ottoman Muslim and Jewish architecture.

I began on my own restoration, using my house as a kind of experiment. Like the other buildings in the Jewish Quarter, it was in disrepair and was deteriorating each winter even more: water was seeping in and collecting in the rubble-fill between walls, foundations had moved, and domes had cracked open.

Breaking through walls required great caution. We would make a little hole, pour some concrete around, make the hole bigger, pour some more concrete, then look around to see if any cracks were forming — literally a trial-and-error process of creating new spaces. I felt a bit like a musician who has been given a melody and asked to base a fugue on it. I knew there was music in those buildings — it was a question of combining their themes in various ways in a kind of architectural canon to a melody that had already been invented.

We began by sealing the cracks in the outer surface and repointing the stonework, but this resulted in the moisture being trapped inside the rubble. Later, when my wife and I took possession of our gleaming new apartment, we found the moisture seeping through the walls, often accompanied by a botanical garden of fungus. Every day, plaster peeled off and a crop of green bacterial moss dropped onto the new furniture and oriental carpets. It was alarming to say the least. Some friends even suggested the bacteria could breed exotic diseases. It took us years to solve the problem, which occurred in many of the renovated houses in the Quarter.

All the existing buildings in Block 38 required extensive work: rebuilding walls, scraping plaster, weaving pipes and wires through the walls, post-tensioning the building together with steel cables, adding a room here and there. Most of the buildings were collections of individual rooms in which whole families had lived, sometimes with four or five families sharing one toilet. We had to convert that kind of accommodation into modern apartments — a living room, two or three bedrooms, a couple of bathrooms. Each became much more than a restoration because as the rebuilt buildings emerged, they took on a new character.

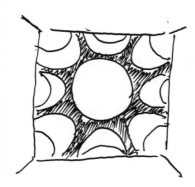

The experience of restoring and adding to the old structures, of grafting the old onto the new, left its mark on me. When I restored the dome in one of my rooms, I realized that the dome, which had been made in the shape of a flower, could have been built in a million ways, some of them quite severe and simple. I enjoyed its flower-like form and I found myself asking about that ingredient of richness which transcends a simple ceiling or the elementary dome.

The discovery that a flower dome holds for me is the recognition of that special imagination, or indulgence, that made the builder deviate from the simplest dome he could have made and elaborate it into a more complex and richer geometry, embellishing, creating ornament and decoration. Now I, as his successor centuries later, lie in my bed and look up at his creation and reflect on the dome above that is segmented to the point where it evokes in me the feeling of a flower. It was surely more than the minimum utilitarian response to the need to build a dome out of small stones.

The dome reminded me of a recent trip through Iran with Nader Ardalan, an Iranian architect friend of many years. We had travelled from one village to another, from one wonderful mosque to another, during which he explained to me that the dome was used because it captured the feelings of Islam about the unity and wholeness of the cosmos.

"Nader, that's nonsense," I told him. "Domes are used because there's no wood in Iran! It evolved in response to the challenge of spanning with brick. It is morphologically inevitable."

The builder of my flower-dome ceiling had to build a dome with small stones because he had no wood for beams. In a wooded part of the country he would have built a flat or inclined roof instead. In Iran, it was obvious as we travelled through areas without access to wood that the buildings had vaulted, arched, or domed ceilings. As soon as we came to the foothills where trees grow, wood beams produced flat ceilings and sloped roofs.

"No, no, no Moshe, you are talking about the evolution of forms like a Darwinian. I don't believe it — either in architecture or in explaining the evolution of the species."

We ended by agreeing that both interpretations could be true. The domes in Iran evolved in response to a need to enclose space with small bricks. But just as in Genesis after every act of creation God paused and appreciated his creation before going on, so in our own human way we made the dome and paused and "saw that it was good." The dome then acquired even greater meaning, being elaborated and enlarged to become the symbolic expression of our communion with God.

To enclose the courtyard in my house, I designed a transparent curved single vault acrylic roof over the courtyard, to keep the space warm in winter and shade it with vines in summer. Then above I added a third level, the living room with its terrace. The idea of terraces brought me face to face with the challenge of seasonally changing spaces.

To be really useful, outdoor space in Jerusalem must be seasonally convertible. In summer, it can become almost intolerably hot. Travelling through Arab districts, one often observes large glazed terraces facing south that are important extensions of the living room in winter — but totally abandoned in summer because they become hot-houses then. In the Arab houses, the family actually migrates from the inner room, which is a summer room, to the outer room, which is a winter room. I was after the same sort of thing — the idea of a convertible space: a space equipped with something that could transform my roof garden into a shaded terrace in the heat of the day, an enclosed terrace in the cool of the evening, and a glazed solarium in the cold and often rainy winter.

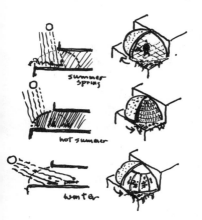

I kept thinking of using domes, echoing the city skyline, but instead of solid ones, transparent ones, bubbles of warmth in the winter sun, somehow trying to make a connection with my convertible Citroën — open in summer and sheltered in winter. This led to the simple idea of a sliding roof — but in the form of a dome? A quarter of a sphere could be in part transparent and in part opaque. And why not let the transparent quarter turn on the axis of the dome? When the dome slid under the opaque quarter, it would create a roofless terrace open to the sky. As the days grew cooler, the transparent dome could be rotated back, as if a door were being closed, thus creating a greenhouse or winter corner — a place with lots of light and sun.

I was very excited about this invention because while it was something completely new in answer to a specific contemporary living problem, it nevertheless made a formal connection to the surroundings. And now if you walk on the Mount of Olives or Mount Scopus and look back on Block 38 and the Old City, you will see this symphony of old and new domes, old and new masses, of similar scale. Take a careful look, however, and the difference can be seen: all the old domes are stone and the new ones are half transparent and half white. The old are heavy, the new, light and bubbly. You are aware that there is a difference — yet it is part of the same melody. It expresses a new element which has to do with life as it is today. It uses modern materials and yet it is connected with the past. It is not just taking a molding detail from the past and arbitrarily plastering it on a new building; it is not taking an architectural detail and using it indiscriminately, out of context. The new domes are counterpoints with the old, they are all in the same key, all variations on the theme of the "musical offering" that the Old City is.

I enjoyed every moment of the restoration of my own house and the other existing buildings on the Block, but the designing of the new buildings which had to fit in between the old ones was a more difficult process. I found myself caught between the multitude of possibilities. When I restored the old buildings I did not feel there was much choice. It was more like a grand seduction. I enjoyed discovering the forms, the shapes and the texture bringing the old buildings to life.

If I had followed the conservative agenda of the Company for the Reconstruction and Development of the Jewish Quarter, things would have been easy. Their recommendation was to rebuild the new buildings to match the old ones, to reproduce their forms and structures and even building techniques. To follow that advice would have been to create a kind of Jerusalem-Williamsburg. Except for the addition of electricity and modern sewers, the Jewish Quarter would have looked as it might have in 1947. That is what the Poles did to the destroyed Warsaw after the Second World War, they made a stage set of the past.

The dilemma set me in the middle of two opposing attitudes: on the one hand, the so-called post-modernists, fascinated by historicism and tradition, and on the other hand, the modernists, optimistically exploring the "brave new world" of sheet metal, glass, plaster and curtain walls. As in most such debates, things were not black and white. It was clear to me that I wanted the new construction to belong, to be part of and in harmony with the old, as with Yeshivat Porat Yosef. The question was whether it could both belong and also be true to itself.

I knew that the scale, colour, and texture of the surrounding area must be preserved, not only because they were beautiful, but because they expressed a domestic scale and life pattern that was still applicable and valid.

I found myself drawing on the experience of Habitat and the yeshiva, proposing large prefabricated concrete wall elements, but here I covered them with thin layers of veneer stone, expressing the concrete at the edges yet taking on the colour of the surroundings. I drew on my experience with my own house, incorporating the convertible domes. The resulting apartments terraced upwards, linking with the existing buildings, incorporating concrete, stone, white dome and acrylic bubbles. Perhaps to some small degree we had achieved the integration of harmony and dissonance I was striving for.

WITH BRUNO ZEVI IN SHIRAZ

While work on Block 38 was in full swing, I was invited to attend a conference of architects convened by Farah Dibah, the Empress of Iran, in Persepolis. Among those who attended was Bruno Zevi, the eminent Italian architect and teacher, a Harvard graduate, editor and then also a broadcaster who ran his own TV station in Rome. Bruno's last name derives from the Hebrew word zvi, which means "deer."

The conference was in the fall and Yom Kippur fell in the middle of it. Zevi and I did not want to let this day pass by uncelebrated. Shiraz, fifteen miles away, one of the most ancient Jewish communities, was settled during the time of the Emperor Cyrus. We managed to get a car and drove through the flat desert, entering Shiraz by the great bazaar where the driver, in despair of understanding where we wanted to go, simply dropped us.

Zevi had been to Israel for meetings of the Jerusalem Committee (of which more later), had seen presentations of several of my sketches and also had visited Porat Yosef. In the committee meetings he was flamboyant, preaching the merits of modernism and the pitfalls of historicism in general terms. Now, he took me to task, saying he was very concerned about my Jerusalem proposals. "What is this eclectic business, this sentimental nonsense of arches and stone walls? What's so wrong with modernity? Every age that built in Jerusalem ignored the past and built its own image. You should have the security and confidence to build in the manner and style of our own time, to put up modern buildings — use steel, concrete and glass!"

I started to explain, when he cut me off — "Look Moshe, Habitat was one of the most significant projects of its era, it opened a new chapter, it exploited contemporary technology. But there, in Jerusalem, you seem to be overwhelmed by tradition and the city's heritage. Be true to yourself! Be a contemporary person, building for contemporary society with contemporary means and contemporary expression."

As we walked through the bazaars, in some vague direction, meandering from one alley to another, each narrower than the one before, our exchange continued.

70

"Bruno," I told him, "where we differ is in the significance of the literal physical setting of a building and the impact that these surroundings and context might have on it. I have my preoccupations with geometry and spatial order, but I am obsessed in Jerusalem with the question of harmony. I have a sense of awe for what is there. I am trying to discover the syntax of the place."

"Moshe," he replied, "it's easy to justify everything in the name of 'the significance of the site' or the pluralism of the local culture. No: it is not a matter of syntax, but of language. Harmony can be achieved only through dissonances, not through assonances, through clear diversities, not through imitations. You are original when you are yourself. You stop being a good architect when you worry about harmony, contextualism, site, monumentality."

"Bruno," I objected, "when you talk about glass and steel buildings in the Old Quarter in Jerusalem, do you mean there's a value and truth in the expressive elements of present day architecture which transcends the setting? Can't you see the contemporary syntax has enormous diversity built into it, letting us manipulate it and mold it so as to achieve harmony with the setting?"

Just then, we heard sounds of unmistakable chanting. And there, in a small square ahead, was a synagogue, with children outside playing.

It was like most Shiraz brick buildings, with decorative trim of geometrical glazed bricks. It had clear windows through which I could see a dome filled with hanging lamps. Although it was very austere from the outside, as we entered we could see an elaborate bimah carved in wood with its canopy on top and the wood and metal inlay Ark where the Torah is kept. It was as if we had gone back in time. The men, many bearded, wore traditional cylinder-shaped hats, white gowns, some of them with stripes. In the gallery, completely separate from the men, slightly veiled by silk hangings, sat the women in embroidered dresses, with long silk shawls covering their heads. We could have been back in the time of Cyrus.

It was by then afternoon and the prayer was nearing its climax. As we entered, a couple of younger men approached us. We seemed to pose a sense of threat to them. Who were we? We identified ourselves: a Jew from Rome, and one from Jerusalem. The room was electrified. Several people came towards us, embraced us, shook our hands, and led us to seats of honor. They spoke He-

71

brew with a Sephardic accent and I had no problem at all communicating with them.

They thought we might want to raise funds for Israel and suggested we make a fund-raising speech. We explained that we just came to be with them and celebrate the holiday. If it had been earlier in the day, they said, when the Torah was out, they would have invited us to an Aliya, the Ascent to the Torah, the greatest of honours.

CHAPTER 6

LIFE IN THE OLD CITY

Now that I had an office and a home in Jerusalem, I began to spend two weeks or more at a time there. The pattern remains the same to this day: every six or eight weeks my family and I go from one world to another. The morning before the trip, we lead the same life as most people do in a big North American city. We live in a house set among trees. I drive to work and go shopping for food a few miles away. Except for the very few things we can do by walking, we accept that most of life's activities require getting into a car and driving.

The evening of a trip, my wife Michal and I load our suitcases and our babies into the car, make our way to the airport, and twelve hours later, in the late afternoon, we find ourselves driving from Tel Aviv airport toward Jerusalem.

We reach Jerusalem just after the sun has set. We enter the city through the Jaffa Gate, at the periphery of the Armenian Quarter, to arrive at the parking area of the Jewish Quarter. And there we are, with the sounds of the new world still in our ears, circling around looking for a parking spot within the ancient city walls.

We unload the baby carriage and babies, the four or five suitcases, and begin the six hundred yard walk down a path, then along Misgav Ladach Street all the way to our home near the Arab market. I can't handle all the cases at once so Michal stays with the babies while I take the first two suitcases. I return, pick up the rest of the bags while Michal gets the babies into the carriage, and off we trot. The stretch from the parking lot to the house is invariably more exhausting than the twelve-hour flight. But when we open the door and go upstairs to the living room, we see all around us the Holy Sepulchre, the Temple Mount, and the Western Wall across the piazza. By now it is dark, so the Wall is brightly floodlit, as are the golden and silver domes of the mosques, the onion domes of the Russian Church of Mary Magdalene, the towers of the Church of the Ascension and Augusta Victoria on the Mount of Olives.

Our house is at the extreme northern end of the Jewish Quarter, two buildings away from the principal east-west Arab market which runs between the Quarters along David Street and the Street of the Chains from the Temple Mount right up to Jaffa Gate. Most Jewish Quarter residents have turned their backs on the life of the Arab markets and get their supplies from the thinly stocked grocery store in the heart of the Jewish Quarter. They do their heavy shopping once a week on Thursdays, the day when the supermarket in downtown Jerusalem reluctantly agrees to deliver to the Jewish Quarter. However, Michal and I have discovered that we can find almost everything we need within a five minute walk to the Arab markets.

The first night we always wake up before dawn to the chant of the muezzin. By the second night we've adjusted and sleep through. At sunrise I go down to the bakery and get bagel bread sprinkled with sesame seeds, or pita, hot from the oven. The vegetable market is open early and I pick up oranges and other fruits in season.

Not far from the vegetable sellers, under vaults which date from twelfth century Crusader times, is a little alcove in the wall where laundry and ironing are done. Just by the crossroads at the bottom of our street is the man who presses his own olives to make the most wonderful dark-green unrefined olive oil, which we consume in quantities and take back to North America.

A few more steps and we pass electrical shops, a hardware store, a metal workshop (where all our copper kitchenware was made), a furniture maker (who made our chairs), a butcher, and so on.

When I go to my office in Mamilla Street, I never take the car. I walk through the market up to Jaffa Gate just as all the shopkeepers are opening. These routine walks have made me an acquaintance, if not a friend, of many of them — all Arabs, some Muslim, some Christian. The ones I know better I greet, shaking hands. The coffee man, carrying on his shoulder the beautiful brass pot with its internal charcoal cylinder to keep the coffee hot, is always there by the gate when I reach the top. I pause and sample this charcoal-tasting coffee before proceeding to the office.

Many of the shops specialize in Palestinian embroidery, dresses and weaving. My love for the craft and its traditions is closely related to my love of Persian carpets and kilims (woven rugs). Michal has a wonderful collection of dresses from Bethlehem, Gaza, Ashdod, Sinai, some even embroidered in Aleppo, the city of my father's birth. Each area has its own particular designs, and we now know the difference between the embroidery which uses natural dyed material and will never fade and dresses made recently with synthetic dyes, which are bright and harshly coloured, run when washed, and fade in the sun.

As we walk through the market, the dress merchant will call us, always offering coffee or mint tea, to show us special pieces that have just arrived. He knows our taste by now and shares with us a sense of connoisseurship. "I have a special new dress," he will say, "with those purples and blues you like so much." Our acquaintanceship has its problems, as I'm no longer as effective a bargainer as I might have been. These dresses (costing around $50 or $60 in 1967) have become more and more scarce as the fellaheen (peasant farmers) and Bedouin dispose of their heirlooms. Nowadays the good ones can't be bought for a thousand dollars.

I often wondered where these dresses came from and how one found the original owners. One day I learned that every Monday morning at five, just before sunrise, the Bedouin and fellahin ladies set up in a little alcove between Christian Quarter Street and David Street. All our local shopkeepers come early and bargain for the dresses.

Early one morning Michal and I got up and surprised our shopkeper friends by joining them.

We felt a strange silence at the beginning; our presence was obviously resented. We examined the merchandise; because I speak

Arabic I could deal with the tough and crotchety old ladies. But the shopkeepers immediately intervened. "Ah, you are interested in that dress? Let me buy it for you." An offer I could not refuse.

Life in the Jewish Quarter — or the Old City — is in some ways the modern North Americans' fantasy of what urban life really could be like. We live in privacy and seclusion but with a view and a sense of the outdoors and we have at our fingertips everything we need for our daily routine. We live in a village with the excitement and choice of a city. On a Saturday, because of the markets, thousands of people come to the Quarter. It takes ten minutes to walk fifty yards; everybody is shoulder to shoulder, tourists, residents, pilgrims, merchants, carts bringing in merchandise. We buy what we need, make our way back to the house, up the stairs, through the door — and there is silence. It is hard to believe that fifty yards away is one of the busiest bazaars in the world.

We sit on the terrace, the whole city is peaceful and silent, and before us is this extraordinary view of the Old City. And yet the distance from the house to the market is no greater than the distance between the house and the end of the property for many suburban residents on their one acre lots.

The alienation between most residents of the Jewish Quarter and the Arab storekeepers in the rest of the Old City is indeed unfortunate. As I said previously, I blame it on the government's ill-advised decision to evict Arab storekeepers from the Jewish Quarter during the restoration. Had they let the existing storekeepers stay on a rental basis, that might have increased the interaction. The people who live in the Jewish Quarter have developed a style of life that focuses primarily on the shopkeepers, banks, and other services provided by the Jews within the Quarter. So while there was a measure of integration before 1948, with the Jews, Muslims, and Christians all doing business together in the markets, the Jews now lead a more or less segregated life.

Another element in the community life of the Jewish Quarter is that, because of the city wall, it is a car-less community. It's a little like Venice in that sense, except that in Venice you've got the vaporettos and gondolas whereas in the Jewish Quarter you have carts and donkeys at best. Since everybody must park at the periphery, we live with the hardship — or benefit, depending on your view — of walking several hundred yards from the closest parking lot.

Reflecting on life in the Old City, one is once again reminded of the overwhelming impact of the car on our cities, indeed our lives. For in the car-driven cities, post–Model T cities — be it Houston or Los Angeles — the accommodation to mobility, roads and freeways and the low densities needed to facilitate parking suggest that access to the diversity of facilities which comprise our daily life is neither spontaneous nor immediate. It forever entails driving. Indeed those in Houston and Los Angeles acknowledge with a sense of resignation that significant parts of their lives are spent driving.

The cities which most approximate the Old City lifestyle are the compact pre-automobile cities. If you live in midtown Manhattan's East Side, on Madison or Third Avenue, you find at the base of your elevator, outside your apartment lobby, every form of convenience — commercial, cultural or otherwise — within easy walking distance. The difference is that for most Manhattanites the trip up the elevator does not lead to a house — a dwelling with a sense of identity, outdoor space or view — but to an apartment, a statistical division of space.

I suppose that it is this conflict between density and compactness and the desire for automobile mobility that has made the traditional life so difficult to achieve today. We must tackle two issues: making habitation within the dense environment better, i.e., transcending the apartment building; and at the other end of the spectrum, compensating for the lost mobility of not having the automobile available instantly with the invention of new modes of transportation.

Living in the Old City, I have also learned that there is an aspect of design, the world of sound, that I had overlooked before. I saw that a certain level of visual privacy could be achieved even at high density. No one looks through my windows and I don't look into anyone else's. But we have not been able to overcome the intrusion of sound as it emanates from the houses — the voices of people, the sound of music, stereos, television sets, bouncing about the walls and alleys. Since the floors and walls of the courtyards are stone, there is high reverberation and not much absorption. Earth absorbs sound but there is little exposed earth in the Old City.

The sounds bounce back in surprising, unexpected ways. For example, the Western Wall is four hundred yards away from our house. On a dark summer's night when the air is cooling and my windows are open, I can hear every word of a man praying in a medium voice, facing the wall with his back to me. At night we can clearly hear the conversation of people walking in the alleys. Sometimes the walls reflect the sound of a mother scolding her child as far as two hundred yards away. Luckily Israel has only one television station, so we don't hear a jumble of different channels playing at the same time. But people adjust: one tones one's voice down in the evening. As darkness descends and the sounds of the markets dissipate, the personal sound level drops too. Old City residents tend not to play their stereos loudly after ten in the evening.

For North Americans, that kind of sharing of acoustical space might seem like a drastic infringement of privacy. The anonymous life of the high-rise tower doesn't entail that kind of association and interaction with the surroundings. But for the Mediterranean soul there is a positive value to the notion that this shared acoustical space makes one part of the community. The presence of neighbors is part of life, and so are all the sounds of the city — the roosters before sunrise, the people praying, the muezzin calling the faithful to prayer, the tolling of church bells. The life of the city comes indoors and forces its way into the awareness. When I put on the stereo I sometimes feel I am not the only one listening but, whether they like it or not, my neighbors are sharing it. This does change with the seasons; during winter windows are shut, making life more introspective and private. But air conditioning is unusual in Jerusalem, so life in summer is more open and interactive.

The other surprise of life in the Jewish Quarter has been the way relations between the diverse groups of the Old City have changed from what we expected in 1967 when we began rebuilding the Quarter. The Company for the Reconstruction and Development of the Jewish Quarter declared as a policy that they would make every effort to have the population of the Jewish Quarter represent a cross-section of Israeli society. Because of that, they did not auction the units to the highest bidders. They realized that would lead to gentrification. Instead they established fair market values and then raffled the units. They also established quotas — so many units to religious families, so many to secular families, so many to families who had lived in the Old City earlier and had roots there, so many to immigrant families. They made it a condition that no one could buy a house in the Quarter except as his principal residence.

In the first few years the population of the Jewish Quarter was heterogeneous, as planned. In time some of the secular families left and were replaced by religious families. There was a natural tendency for religious people to concentrate because of the many yeshivot — Porat Yosef, Yeshivat Hakotel, Yeshivat Aish Ha Torah, and others — and naturally the teachers and students gravitate toward the Old City. But with the years the turnover accelerated.

Right now there are very few secular families living in the Old City. The fear of tension between the Jewish and Arab families in the Old City has proved to be baseless thus far. Relations are reasonable unless external circumstances force it to be otherwise. In contrast, relations between the Orthodox and secular Jews in the Quarter are strained.

This is not to say that relations between any of the groups in Jerusalem are stable. Between Arab and Jew both external or internal events can bring about abrupt change (a regional war, a fire in the mosques, an Arab guerilla attack can rapidly destroy the status quo). Among the Jews in the Quarter, indeed the city, there is an uncertainty as the residents of Jerusalem get caught in the conflict between secular and Orthodox Jews, those who see the future of the country as either a secular democracy or a clerical autocracy.

CHAPTER 7

ARCHAEOLOGICAL OBSTACLES AND DELIGHTS

One morning when excavations were under way for the construction of Yeshivat Porat Yosef, the bulldozers uncovered a series of large clay tubes that led to a carved channel in the bedrock. We were clearly in the Herodian strata and the tubes were part of the aqueduct system which had brought water to the Temple two thousand years ago.

Every Old City construction project in Jerusalem is carried out in an atmosphere of tension and anxiety over the possible uncovering of archaeological remains under the structure. Discoveries such as this aqueduct system would invariably entail alterations of plans, and the increased costs could be tremendous. In fact, when we began excavation for the yeshiva, the rabbis insisted that we accelerate the process and get the bulldozers moving fast enough so that no ancient remnant would be noticed even if uncovered.

The antiquities law, initially enacted under the British Mandate, is unequivocal in giving complete authority to the Department of Antiquities over all archaeological remains found within the country. The financial burden for excavation and preservation of these remains often falls upon the owner of the land. It is assumed to be one of those responsibilities one accepts as part of the cost of building in the Holy City, but it has compounded the problems of restoring old buildings in the Jewish Quarter. All of the Old City has been declared an antiquity zone, which means that before any land-owner, including the government, is allowed to build, the Department of Antiquities has the right to excavate and explore what is under the site. If the dig uncovers anything of significance, the Department of Antiquities has the right to require either complete preservation and the cancellation of any building plans; alternatively it can demand that the new building be redesigned so that the archaeological find can be preserved beneath it.

To our relief and surprise the only remnant found on the eastern side of the yeshiva site was that small section of the Herodian aqueduct, which collapsed under the onslaught of the bulldozers before anybody had a chance to say much about it. At that moment we thought we were home free because this was the part of the site facing the Western Wall, where we were most likely to find significant remains.

Then we uncovered a large Crusader vault and a couple of other structures that were probably from the Crusader era. Professor Nahman Avigad, the archaeologist in charge, came to the site, examined the Crusader structures, saw to it that they were properly documented, and said that they were not of sufficient significance to affect us. We could go ahead and demolish them.

Some months after we began to pour our foundations, I was on my way to the yeshiva to inspect the construction and found myself distracted by a commotion across the public stairs. On a site where several houses were to be built, the apse of an important Crusader church had been unearthed. Avigad and several other archaeologists were there, in the midst of a great deal of excitement. The outline of the church was almost complete.

It was immediately decided not to build houses on that site at the edge of Block 38, but to leave the area open; eventually it was restored as an archaeological garden with the remnants of the church partially reconstructed. Mayor Teddy Kollek felt it was important to demonstrate Israel's commitment to the restoration of the archaeological remnants of all cultures and all periods.

For some time there was a sign on the church reading "Remnants of the Church of Holy Mary of the German Knights," but the religious zealots of the Old City continually defaced the sign because of its Christian connection. So it now says "Archaeological Garden." But there it is, no matter what the name, a Teutonic church, right in the middle of the Jewish Quarter.

Several months later, next door to our site, on the site where Yeshivat Hakotel was being built, the builders uncovered several rooms of a Herodian building of palatial scale. We began to feel surrounded. The eastern side of our site was well under way, but there was still considerable excavation to be done on the western part, right next to the Yeshivat Hakotel, where our plans called for a swimming pool and gymnasium. The Herodian structure must inevitably extend into our site.

We had a number of meetings with the site superintendent, but the archaeologists warned us not to allow our bulldozers into the areas before they had done some hand excavation. Three weeks later, it had become clear that we were sitting right on top of a major find. The walls of one room of the palace seemed to be intact all the way up to the ceiling level, with frescoes still in good condition. The swimming pool in our plan was to occupy the same space, so without major modifications we would not be allowed to proceed.

For a while I had a dream of trying to incorporate the pool into the Herodian room and make the fresco part of the decor, but we would have had to put in major foundation walls to support not only the pool but also the dining room and five storeys of dormitories above it. It was impossible.

A meeting was held at the offices of the Company for the Reconstruction and Development of the Jewish Quarter to decide what to do about the palace and the two yeshivas that were under construction. Nahman Avigad opened the meeting with an emotional speech about the importance of the discovery. One of the rooms, he said, had been found black with ashes, showing that the house had been burnt during the destruction of the city by Titus in A.D. 70.

What could be done? Both buildings would have to rise above the archaeology, literally and figuratively. Big concrete columns in clear areas within the ruins would support the structures spanning above, and continuous archaeological restoration would extend two or three hundred feet under both buildings. The palace would become an important part of the meandering archaeological under-city of Jerusalem.

Although disappointed at losing the swimming pool, I decided to seize this new opportunity to design a library in the area abutting the archaeological remains. An uninterrupted glass wall would follow the undulating edge of the remains so that one could sit in the library and look out onto the archaeological excavations lit by shafts open to the sky.

Needless to say, the cost of all this was enormous. Both buildings had to be redesigned, which meant new working drawings and new structural and mechanical drawings. The large distances that had to be spanned added greatly to the construction cost. I have come to believe that the antiquities law is unhealthily skewed in the favor of the archaeologists, who can demand all sorts of splendid things for which they don't have to put up the funds. It doesn't seem reasonable that the archaeologist should be given such unrestricted powers without having to bear the financial consequences.

The problems were compounded because the government wanted to restore the Jewish Quarter and get it inhabited as quickly as possible, for political reasons. Ideally, sites should have been excavated before buildings were designed. Findings could have been documented, the criteria for preservation outlined, and only then would the architect begin his designs. But the Company could not afford to wait two or three years to begin construction, and it instructed the architects to proceed with plans while the archaeologists dug.

I was involved in another archaeological discovery in 1973 when I was restoring a group of buildings known as the Hosh at the western end of the Jewish Quarter on the Street of the Jews. The street itself had been the subject of an architectural competition (which I had entered) won by Israeli architects Peter Bugod, Ester Niv, and Shlomo Aronson.

When Bugod and his team began to excavate for the new buildings, they came upon some very large stones set in a familiar Roman pattern. Clearly it was the paving of a principal Roman street. This caused great excitement. People thought it might be the Cardo that was shown on a Byzantine mosaic map unearthed in Jordan, known as the Madaba Map. (Our knowledge of fourth to seventh century Jerusalem is based mostly on this map.)

On the mosaic map the Cardo appears to be some sixty feet wide, with pairs of columns on each side, but over the years scholars have regarded this as an exaggeration of the artist, finding it difficult to believe that this small provincial Roman city (Jerusalem) could have been of such importance to warrant structures equal to those found in Rome at the time.

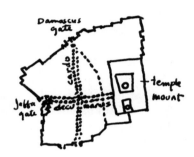

Roman cities were usually bisected by two main streets, the Cardo and the Decumanus, which met in the form of a cross. Roman Jerusalem eventually evolved into a Byzantine city (hence the map), to be rebuilt in turn by the Umayyad Muslims around the seventh century, then by the Crusaders in the eleventh and twelfth centuries, followed immediately by the Mamelukes (who were actually a nation of Muslim former slaves from Egypt) and finally the Ottoman Turks. This process piled building upon building, layer upon layer, but the Old City is still divided by streets in a cross axis as the Roman city was, making the four Quarters: Arab, Christian, Armenian and Jewish.

Having uncovered the paving stones, the archaeologists slowly and carefully began to dig toward the Hosh, where, according to the map, they should find the colonnade. Sure enough, as soon as they reached the edge of the Hosh, they discovered the bases of the colonnade of magnificent columns and capitals.

If this was the Cardo, then on the opposite side a similar buried colonnade should exist. They dug down sixty feet to the east, the presumed width of the Cardo according to the Madaba map, and again there it was! Then they drew a straight line toward Damascus

Gate, went along it for two or three hundred feet, into a vacant lot, dug down, and once more hit the great Cardo.

During the following three years, careful rebuilding and restoration turned the Cardo into a market street with shops on both sides, apartments above them, all supported by enormous vaults. This new bazaar is several feet lower than the adjacent Street of the Jews, the architects having cleverly played one level against the other.

One sunny spring day in 1973, my friends Charles and Barbara Bronfman arrived in Jerusalem. They were old friends of Teddy Kollek as well as supporters of the Israel Museum and many other projects in the city. Teddy was taking them on a tour, giving them an update on what was happening in the city, and he asked that I join them.

As we walked around the city wall, we paused at Jaffa Gate and spent a few moments discussing Mamilla, which Charles knew well from previous visits. We walked on along the narrow cobbled street between the high walls of the Armenian Quarter towards the Jewish Quarter's temporary parking area. We stopped at an adjacent vacant lot which dropped steeply toward the city wall — the only vacant area on this side of the Old City. As we watched carts pulled by little tractors and donkeys dump their fill and construction debris, Teddy mentioned the speculation that an amphitheatre might have existed there in Roman times. He added that there were not enough parks and playgrounds for the residents of the Jewish Quarter today.

"We must invent something new," Teddy said, "a garden theatre, a park with playgrounds that can also be used for performances. Last week we had a concert in the square in front of Deutscher Platz. There were hundreds of people — it was wonderful! We need a more permanent facility. There could be concerts, plays, films. The Old City needs it badly — and its residents even more so."

I picked up on Teddy's vibes. This was not just a casual briefing. Teddy was on the "sell," proposing a project to Charles. Charles, accustomed to propositions of all kinds, listened with reserved interest. Barbara was enthusiastic. Teddy was ready with estimates of construction for the project. It was assumed I would design it.

"Of course," I responded, "I would be happy to."

Charles smiled. "Can it be ready in two years for my son Stephen's bar mitzvah?"

"No problem," I said. "It should be a fairly straightforward construction. Then the bar mitzvah ceremony can take place during the inauguration." Thus the project was born, and as we continued walking around the wall, this new idea churned in my mind.

I developed sketches, getting more and more excited as I managed to find a way of combining a garden with an amphitheatre. Terraces accommodating playgrounds would become like balconies in a theatre looking down onto the stage.

As soon as the plans were ready, the bulldozers were to begin by removing the debris and excavating down to the level of the stage. After the experience of the yeshiva, we were nervous about archaeological discoveries that might affect the plans. So I asked Professor Nahman Avigad about the likelihood of finding anything. He said that to the best of his knowledge the chances were small and in any event, he was not aware of anything specific we should look for.

So we sent in the bulldozers. Down they went — ten feet, twenty feet, thirty feet, forty feet, fifty feet, the level of the stage — nothing! We heaved great sighs of relief; a clear site after all! I reported to the Mayor that here was the exception to the rule — a clear site ready to build.

The following day, as the bulldozer was lumbering out of the site, its blade caught on something and uncovered a small hole about two feet in diameter.

The foreman called my office. I nervously trotted over, got down on my knees, and peered into the darkness through the small opening. We dropped in some stones, but we could not hear them land. We lowered a workman on a rope, and as he went down and down we realized that the void was more than fifty feet deep.

When the man finally landed below, he let out a shout of surprise. There were four enormous vaults fifty feet high and sixty feet long, all fully stuccoed and built with the alternating layers of brick and stone commonly found in Byzantine architecture.

Professor Avigad came over, very excited, and investigated. This was no ordinary residential building; it took us down more than a hundred feet below the surface of the Jewish Quarter. He suggested it might be the lower level of the sixth century Nea Church, or New Church of St. Mary, one of the two great churches found on the Madaba Map, the other being the Church of the Holy Sepulchre. The latter is in use today but no physical traces had remained of the Nea, shown on the map at the opposite, southern end. Like the Cardo, it had always remained somewhat of a mystery; perhaps it had merely been an unrealized plan. So if this was really the Nea, we would be confirming a very important fact in the history of Byzantine Jerusalem.

Avigad's suspicion that this really was the Nea was reinforced when one hundred yards away, under another part of the Old City, he uncovered the bases and capitals of two very large Ionic columns. These too, he speculated, might be part of the Nea.

Almost the entire gift Charles Bronfman had originally pledged was used for excavation. After several months of picking through and carting off the debris, we found on the wall of this great vaulted space a Greek inscription that confirmed it was indeed the lower level of the Nea.

And this is the work which our most pious Emperor Flavius Justinianus carried out with munificence, under the care and devotion of the most Holy Constantinus, Priest and Hegumen, in the thirteenth year of the indiction.

We measured up the excavation and drew a map that vividly shows the six interconnected vaults.

By coincidence, a few weeks later, I went to the annual Jerusalem International Book Fair and found a copy of the classic work about Jerusalem written and illustrated by the great British archaeologist Charles Warren, who uncovered a good part of the city in the nineteenth century. Leafing through, I discovered a sketch of these

very vaults! It was captioned, "Unidentified vaults at the edge of the city wall at Birket el-Kabrit," which indicated that Warren had reached these vaults, measured, and recorded them a hundred years earlier. He didn't identify them as the Nea, and in the hundred years that had passed since he saw them, construction fill and other debris had been dumped in the area and must have covered up the access.

We were not about to let pass this opportunity to embarrass the archaeologists. We pointed out that if they had been a little more careful in their research, we would have known about the vaults before we began designing. Not only would our design have accommodated this from the outset, but a lot of money would have been saved.

A discovery of this magnitude meant we would have to completely revamp our plans. What had been a half million dollar garden theatre now became a huge restoration project for the Nea, with perhaps an amphitheatre floating above it. Thus developed a major battle. There were those who said that the amphitheatre and gardens should be abandoned and that we should simply restore the vaults and open them to the public. Because he was extremely concerned over the lack of play space and greenery for the residents of the Jewish Quarter, the Mayor supported the opposing view that our garden should be built over the vaults.

It was eventually decided that I should develop plans for a multi-layered, three-dimensional scheme, with the Nea below and the garden and theatre above. Large openings would illuminate the vaults and allow one to look down into them from the garden above. But with planning procedures being what they are in Jerusalem, there were many people who had to review the design: first the Department of Antiquities and Professor Avigad; then the consulting architects to the Department of Antiquities; and finally the Municipal Planning Committee and their consultig architects. For four years, we designed, negotiated, redesigned, renegotiated, drawing up four complete alternatives with scores of minor variations. By then not only had Charles Bronfman's son Stephen gone through his bar mitzvah — I was getting worried we wouldn't make it for his wedding!

We made progress with the design reviews, but then in 1978, a new problem arose. The Orthodox religious factions in the city were battling with the Mayor over the location of the sports stadium. The original site was opposed by the religious groups because it was close to their neighborhoods, and they feared that the use of it on Saturdays would prevent proper observance of the Sabbath. As part of their strategy, they also objected to the idea of an amphitheatre in the Jewish Quarter. "Who knows," they said, "what uses such an amphitheatre might encourage? Plays and concerts today, perhaps, but tomorrow there could be rock music or a discotheque. It might even be used on the Sabbath!" The Mayor, in an attempt to neutralize this particular issue, pressed us to minimize the number of seats, eliminate the projection room and other theatre facilities, and cease calling the project an "amphitheatre," calling it instead a "garden." We redesigned again.

At last in 1980, I came up with a plan that seemed to satisfy everyone. The collapsed vaults of the Nea would be rebuilt in concrete, thus re-creating the entire space as it was in Byzantine times. A copy of the inscription, which by then had been moved for protection to the Israel Museum, would be placed on the walls, and we would try to find some use for the subterranean space, perhaps as a hall for chamber music. And above would be the garden and the theatre.

Teddy Kollek was still trying to reassure the religious factions that what we were planning was now nothing more than a garden. But the Orthodox continued to fight the project, and at one point, Teddy gave in. One morning as I walked towards the parking area where I keep my car, I saw a truck from the Municipal Landscape Department next to the amphitheatre site. Laborers were bringing down little cypress trees and ficus plants in cans and laying them over the concrete foundations of the amphitheatre in a futile attempt to make it into a garden.

By then Charles Bronfman was really discouraged and discontinued his sponsorship, telling the Mayor he no longer wanted to be involved. So after six years of toil and negotiations, work on the amphitheatre came to a standstill.

Throughout the process of rebuilding the Jewish Quarter, we could not help wondering whether the demands of the archaeologist to save every remnant were not excessive.

Today a visitor to Jerusalem may come to Jaffa Gate and go directly into the Citadel, which has been excavated and converted into a museum. Here, the artifacts and the exhibits are totally integrated with the remains of the structure. Ottoman mosques, Mameluke remains, Herodian walls and rooms — one can move through them all, layer by layer.

Imagine a subterranean city where you can move through the layers of Jebusite, First Temple, Herodian, Roman, Byzantine, Umayyad, Crusader, Mameluke and Ottoman buildings, with a new and living Jewish Quarter floating above them supported by a forest of tall pillars, like one of those cities described by Italo Calvino in *Invisible Cities* (Marco Polo's tales of places on his visit to Kublai Khan). Sunlight pours through to the city underneath. Children descend through hidden stairs into the lower city, visit Herodian palaces, walk along the Roman Cardo, play war games in the headquarters of the Tenth Legion, sneak through the Byzantine waterworks, and ascend back to their homes dreaming of treasures discovered below, little pots with gold coins, jewellery and glassware. Each trip becomes a voyage of discovery into the history of their city. At certain moments, it seemed we were about to bring one of Calvino's fantasies into reality.

Builders and architects in the Jewish Quarter, myself included, frequently complain about the archaeologists. "Oh, they're at us again. They're making us change plans again, delaying us again." But when one walks through the Old City and the Jewish Quarter today, after twenty years of restoration and renovation, and one actually sees the results of their tenacity, these efforts take on a different light. Thus in Jerusalem today, all those unique archaeological remains, each preserved as the result of its own individual battle, have now been linked up and their sum total is much greater than each individual part.

CHAPTER 8

A BRIDGE BETWEEN COMMUNITIES

One day in 1972 I was working on the yeshiva in our new offices in the Jewish Quarter when my secretary came in to say that Eliezer Ronnen, an important city councillor, had dropped in unannounced.

I knew of him: born in Mexico, he had immigrated to Israel, settled on a kibbutz and became involved in the political party MAPAM, a leftist faction of labour. A close adviser to Mayor Teddy Kollek, he had just been appointed chairman of Karta, the newly formed Central Jerusalem Development Company.

Given his background, I expected the typical kibbutz socialist, dressed in an open-collared white shirt with khaki slacks. Instead, in walked a heavy-set man with graying hair, a Stalinesque moustache and an enormous Havana cigar. His loose-fitting brown suit was set off by a striped silk necktie. Peering over his rimless glasses, gesturing broadly, and smoking that cigar, he looked like a Latin American tycoon. Some American developers I knew later nicknamed him Trotsky. When he spoke, everything was a declaration or exclamation. But even when he was angry, he smiled.

Ronnen introduced himself and sat down. "You know that no man's land outside Jaffa Gate?"

"You mean Mamilla?" The word probably comes from the Arabic Moi min Allah, meaning "water from God," referring to the pools and cisterns in the Valley of Hinnom, the traditional western reservoir of water for Jerusalem.

"Yes. We've decided it's got to be completely redeveloped. I'm approaching five of the leading Israeli firms of architects and urban designers. Would you be interested?"

It was a little like that first moment when I walked near the Western Wall and saw the ruins of the yeshiva, but this time I felt even greater emotion: fifty years earlier, one of my relatives had tried to develop that same site, and it had led to his death.

My great-uncle Eliyahu Shamah (the grandfather of Yaffa, wife of the yeshiva's Rabbi Moshe Shrem) had bought the southern section of Mamilla in the 1920s. He believed it would be a good location for Arabs and Jews to do business together, furthering amicable relations between them. He conceived and constructed what came to be called the "new commercial center," a group of two and three storey workshops and offices halfway between the Arab markets of the Old City and the newly emerging business district in downtown Jerusalem.

He invested his entire fortune in the center. But just as it began operation in 1929, tensions increased between the two communities. On August 24, 1929, the Mufti of Jerusalem preached a fanatically nationalist sermon on the Temple Mount. His hysterical congregation came raging out of the city gates and headed in various directions, including Mamilla. In a number of districts, demonstrations occurred and Jews were slaughtered.

As a result of this violence, Mamilla was more or less abandoned, and my great-uncle's dream of creating a centre to bring the two communities together failed. He lost his fortune and went into bankruptcy; shortly thereafter, in deep depression, he died, having fallen off a roof. He is presumed to have taken his own life.

Now, Eliezer Ronnen was asking me if I would be interested in working on Mamilla. My excitement for the opportunities of the site were mixed with concern, particularly about the complex bureaucracy of the planning network. Would I spend months creating exciting proposals only to be stopped dead in my tracks by the skeptical planning authorities?

I proposed some conditions. My Montreal office was then completing the master plan for Coldspring New Town in Baltimore. There, we had held regular meetings with all city departments, so they could become familiar with every aspect of the plan as it evolved and feel a commitment to it. I asked Ronnen to let me do the same in Jerusalem. Second, I wanted to make the planning process open to the public. Then they too would feel part of the process.

The second proposal brought a smile. "You've been working here for two or three years, but you're still naive if you think you can have the kind of public participation there is in America. However, if you want to try it, I have no objections." Ronnen immediately asked the chief "city engineer" (a title left over from the British Mandate; he is actually chief planning officer) to set up the biweekly meetings and assign personnel.

A week later Ronnen called to congratulate us. We had been appointed architects for Mamilla.

I immediately began thinking and dreaming about the site. Whatever was built there had to connect Arab and Jew, Old City and new. But what character, therefore, should it have? Should it be a park? A park does not bring people together. Perhaps the kind of connection that really brings people together had been foreseen by my great-uncle — an urban center, a mixture of retail, recreational, and cultural facilities, hotels, and office space.

I knew that proposing this would touch a raw nerve in many quarters of the city. A commercial centre near the city wall? A place of business for Arabs and Jews near a national park? A major intervention next to the old city? All of these were taboos in Jerusalem.

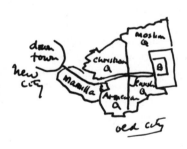

Mamilla's past was heavily marked by the 1948 War of Independence. The armistice agreement brought about a circuitous north-south border, cutting Mamilla, and the city as a whole, in two. The walled Old City, with all the holy places, was within the Jordanian half. The agreement stipulated that Israelis would have access to the Jewish holy places in the Old City, but this stipulation was not honored. The modern downtown, which stretched along the Jaffa road westward from the Old City and had served all the city's residents, both Arabs and Jews, was in the Israeli half, so Arabs created their own business district to the east.

The border dividing the city had consisted of walls and barbed wire, with a demilitarized zone on either side. These zones had rapidly been abandoned or had deteriorated into slums due to the continual sniping and border skirmishes. For the residents of each side, the other half of the city was almost nonexistent; only U.N. personnel and some diplomats crossed the border through the Mandelbaum Gate.

On the Arab side of Jerusalem, little was built during the years between 1948 and 1967. Access was difficult, so tourism was limited, and the capital of Jordan, Amman, was 40 miles away. The eastern half of Jerusalem had stagnated.

On the Israeli side, things had been quite different: vast numbers of immigrants had had to be absorbed, and new neighborhoods had been thrown up, changing the face of the city. Israeli planners had thought nothing of putting up high-rise buildings. When criticized later, they claimed that they had not had access to the Mount of Olives and so could not see how terrible the Old City looked against a backdrop of hotel and office towers. If nothing else, high-rise buildings had allowed Israelis to see the Old City over the dividing walls.

My wife, Michal, was born in Jerusalem in 1951. She grew up in a nineteenth century house with a walled garden, a five minute walk from Damascus Gate and the border. Three hundred yards from her house, at the bottom of the Street of the Prophets, was a high wall and barbed wire. Five hundred yards beyond that wall was another world: the markets of the Old City, the hustle and bustle of the Arab central business district. Villagers in the Old City arrived by bus and taxi from all over the West Bank; Muslim and Christian pilgrims came to worship. All of this activity, this culture, was nonexistent for Michal and her generation. She had no sense of the architecture, of the smells, spices, of the markets — only hints, when for example at night she heard the muezzin chant, not knowing quite what to make of it.

It is difficult for those who have not lived in a divided city — Berlin or Jerusalem — to comprehend that two parallel cultures can coexist within a distance of a few metres with minimal awareness of one another. The Jerusalem of Michal's childhood was a homo-

Mamilla —
The site of Mamilla, 1986.
In the background is Jaffa Gate
and the Temple Mount.
At the bottom right
is the Hebrew Union College
under construction.
The Valley road is already
under construction.
(Werner Braun)

Mamilla — An etching of the pools of Mamilla and Jaffa Gate, 19th century.

Mamilla — The chaos of parking and traffic by Jaffa Gate.

Mamilla — The series of concrete barricades constructed along Mamilla Street as protection from snipers, 1948 – 1967.

Mamilla — The protective wall separating Mamilla from the "No man's land," 1948 – 1967.

Mamilla — Mamilla standing desolate, after the relocation of residents and businesses, 1985.

Mamilla — The original model for the 1974 plan, with the Valley of Hinnom as a park. Residences and a hotel are to the left, the Mamilla mall and parking to the right.

Mamilla — Model of the revised Mamilla plan. The valley road has been incorporated into the park with buildings along the north side of Mamilla Street slated for restoration.
(David Harris)

Mamilla — View of Mamilla Street today.

Mamilla — Mamilla Street, as proposed in the plan. Restoration to the left; new construction to the right. *(Michael Guran)*

The entrance to Mamilla, current conditions.

The entrance to Mamilla as proposed in the plan. *(Michael Guran)*

Mamilla — The proposed piazza and grand steps leading to the shopping passage atop the parking garage. The traffic runs below and is separated from the pedestrians. *(Michael Guran)*

Mamilla — The promenade leading to Jaffa Gate from the City Hall piazza; the parking garage and mall are below the landscaped promenade on the right. *(Michael Guran)*

geneous town with a single culture, isolated and provincial. Life was similarly narrow for the Arab residents on the Jordanian side.

On the seventh day of the Six Day War, the bulldozers tore down the wall and the barbed wire. Michal and her family walked down to Damascus Gate and through it to the markets of the Old City. They wandered through the alleys, among the Ottoman buildings, seeing their newly discovered neighbors. At age 16, a native of Jerusalem, she discovered for the first time the East: a new culture, a new people.

In 1967, the two cul-de-sac cities were joined together becoming again a crossroads for the region, and with this event came a much richer life. Suddenly the sleepy mood was transformed as the Jews and Arabs met in the streets and the markets. Once again, coexistence became a live issue. But the no man's land of Mamilla was still depressingly untouched.

As always, before I even thought of approaching the design problem, I visited the site, walking, looking and listening. Standing outside Jaffa Gate I could see the city walls to the north and south, the result of one of the most visionary of Mayor Teddy Kollek's plans: immediately after the 1967 reunification of Jerusalem, he removed all the buildings clinging to the outside of the city walls. The whole area from Damascus Gate to Jaffa Gate had been cleared of buildings and landscaped, so the impressive ramparts, hidden by the last century of haphazard building, were once again open to view.

Jaffa Gate is one of seven working gates that serve the walled city, and traditionally it is the principal entrance for pilgrims, facing as it does the west toward Jaffa on the coast. In Arabic, it is Bab el Halil, Gate of Hebron, as it begins the main route to that city, which is beyond Bethlehem to the south.

Jaffa Gate is also, unfortunately, the main gate through which vehicles enter the Old City. In 1898, when the Ottomans were in control, Kaiser Wilhelm II came on a state visit to Jerusalem as the guest of the Sultan, Abdulhamid II, and the embankment in front of the gate was demolished to enable the Kaiser to enter the Old City in his coach. This opened the Old City to vehicles. A baroque clock tower was built on top of the gate in 1907 but was removed by the British in the 1920s after they had taken Jerusalem. They left the roadway through the gate, however. When I stood in front of the Gate in 1971, the area was clear of buildings but was filled instead with hundreds of cars, buses, and trucks. What had been designated as a park was in fact an expanse of asphalt, motor vehicles, and garbage.

That day my usual confrontation with the heavy Mamilla Street traffic took on a new significance. The inconvenience I had taken for granted in the past when I tried to cross the street now became a design challenge. Surely, whatever the plan was, I would have to resolve this impossible conflict for the thousands of pedestrians pouring in and out of the city.

I looked westward across the Valley of Hinnom, which bisected Mamilla. Together with the Kidron Valley to the east, it defined the Old City and in ancient times formed part of the defensive attributes of the site. Designated as a national park in 1967, the lower part of the Valley of Hinnom was now lavishly landscaped, but the upper part, within Mamilla, had been filled in, levelled, and built over between 1900 and 1948. (In general the British planning controls protecting historic valleys had been quite strict, but the filling-in had begun during Ottoman rule.) There was something strangely incongruous about its lavish topography — olive trees and terraces, pools and fig trees were suddenly interrupted by dilapidated two and three storey buildings, only to resume five hundred metres to the west on the higher level as Independence Park. The whole valley would have to be restored, I decided. We'd have to remove buildings, dig out landfill, rebuild terraces and replant the olive and fig orchards. I wondered if the pools of water could even be restored and refilled with water.

With my decision to re-create the valley and keep it as an open space, the plan of Mamilla was almost designing itself. The original topography was giving me clues, as it usually did, generating the urban design concept.

Pleased with the ideas that were growing so readily, I walked along Mamilla Street, noticing on my right the nineteenth century monastery and orphanage of St. Vincent de Paul set back from a walled garden, behind a row of boarded-up shops. I read the signs: "Property of Karta — Mamilla Redevelopment." On my left, blocking my view of the valley, was a chaotic row of mostly three storey stone buildings from this century.

I went down the public stairs to the valley bottom and crossed to the southern side, which had first been developed by my great-uncle. Here I found myself in what had become a real slum. Some of the workshops were boarded up, but many were still in use as body shops and garages. Mechanics were working in the streets; the workshops behind were filled with parts. Families lived above the shops, and children played between the cars and on the roofs. Laundry covered every roof and wall. Makeshift extensions of wood and tin provided additional rooms, kitchens and, in some cases, washrooms.

I stopped and chatted with people. One group said they had a single bathroom for four families. They also shared one kitchen. Four children lived in one room, a family of ten in two.

I reached the top of the ridge and looked up to see the King David Hotel, which marked the end of Mamilla. I then turned around and headed back toward Jaffa Gate. I passed the Tannous Brothers Building, named after the developers who constructed it at the turn of the century. A famous Israeli stronghold, it faced what had been the no-man's land and it was pock-marked with bullet holes, a memorial to the wars of 1948 and 1967 and the shooting matches in between. Forty-six families, all of Moroccan origin, now lived in its ten apartments. Decorated windows in an upper floor indicated a community synagogue. Half a dozen children and women occupied each of the many entrances along the sidewalk. Life on the street was more comfortable than in the buildings.

I reached Jaffa Gate once again and paused for a last look around. Mamilla's buildings were clearly products of this century and, with all due respect to my great-uncle, not very significant architecturally or physically — not much character there, I thought. No, opening up the valley must be my real priority, so with the exception of the monastery, the adjacent church and shops, I felt the other buildings in Mamilla should be demolished, the pock-marked Tannous building along with them.

As the master plan developed, I did propose restoring the entire valley to its original level and turning it into a public park. On either side, the slopes would be covered with terraced buildings that increased in steepness, ranging from two storey buildings at the bottom to some seven storeys on the ridges. The southern ridge, connecting to the King David Hotel, would be largely residential and include a hotel. The northern, connecting to the downtown business district, would contain retail and office space. Most important of all, in order to separate cars and people, I proposed to excavate the Mamilla and Jaffa streets one floor below their present level. In the Jaffa Gate area I proposed a 600 car parking structure, a bus terminal, and a merchandise depot to serve the Old City. I would put a pedestrian mall forming a continuous thousand foot long suq (market) over it which would extend along Mamilla Street and would link the Old City markets with the downtown shopping area.

The new plan for Mamilla would necessitate designing a new network of roads, eliminating the small streets, one of which was named after my great-uncle, Eliyahu Shamah Street. He was much in my thoughts — would the new Mamilla confirm his dream half a century later? I was determined to see to it that the new boulevard be named after him.

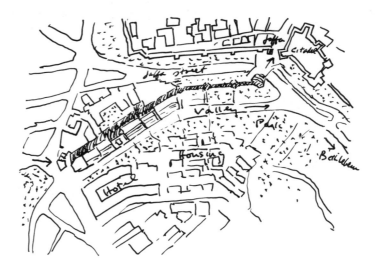

THE JERUSALEM COMMITTEE

The first city plan for the united and enlarged Jerusalem was produced in 1970. Its proposals were far-reaching and Mayor Teddy Kollek established the Jerusalem Committee to review the plan. The committee included renowned theologians, scholars, architects, and planners from around the world, such as Buckminster Fuller, Louis Kahn, Nikolaus Pevsner, Bruno Zevi and Lawrence Halprin.

To this day, the committee members, some Jewish and some not, come to Jerusalem every few years, review what is going on, and give their advice to the Mayor.

Until the initial meeting of the Jerusalem Committee in 1970, my own involvement in the city was limited primarily to the designs of the Manchat community, Porat Yosef, and the Jewish Quarter. I had not yet focused on the region as a whole.

The master plan produced by the city administration was the first attempt to cope with the rapid growth of the city and its consequences for transportation. It was also the first plan to cover the entire region, and it was the first to try to accommodate a population projected to grow to nearly a million by the year 2000.

The planners assumed that most residents fifteen to twenty years hence would be using private vehicles as their main means of transportation, even for trips to the city center. As a result, their plan had the character of a typical U.S. city plan, with a grid of many expressways running from north to south and from east to west.

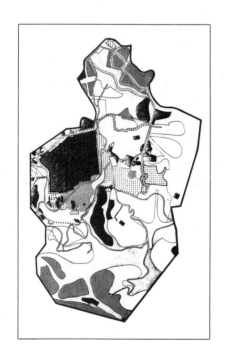

In order to weave this system of roads through the city, they proposed some radical (or preposterous, depending on your point of view) changes to the city fabric. In addition to the expressways, a whole series of road widenings were proposed. The main shopping street, Jaffa Street, was to be widened, knocking out a whole string of buildings. Similarly, the Street of the Prophets was to be widened, shaving off the edge of the historic Ethiopian Quarter.

Even if the plan had achieved formal approval, the city and the government of Israel could never have carried it out, for economic reasons alone. The cost of expropriating the land and buildings would have been beyond any imaginable budget. But the transportation planners would certainly have implemented those parts of the plan that were in the path of least resistance.

Most of the residents of Jerusalem at the time had been unaware of the plan or were unable to understand or respond to it. The presentation to the Committee was perhaps the first detailed description of the plan's intentions.

It was a delicate moment. The Committee members felt they were Kollek's personal guests and yet they wanted to speak out against a plan that his own administration had produced. They were nervous about hurting the Mayor politically, nervous about hurting the municipality of Jerusalem in the international press. My own position was also touchy. Since I was both an Israeli and part of the international constituency, and I had worked with or known many of the people on the Committee, they looked to me for guidance. I was indignant about the plan. My reactions may have antagonized some of the planners who had drawn it up, but Teddy Kollek respected the Committee's right to express its views on the matter.

The Committee strongly recommended that this first plan should be reconsidered, particularly its transportation proposals; that neighborhoods deserving preservation should be defined; that the road system must acknowledge the historic heritage of the city, even at the expense of making it difficult to drive into some parts of the city.

It was Bruno Zevi who said, with flamboyant Italian-accented oratory, "This is not just any city. This is Jerusalem, this is a very special city. Any plan must express its specialness!"

CHAPTER 9

I DISCOVER A GREAT URBAN DESIGNER

On the first day of the Six Day War, June 5, 1967, the Jordanians began shooting across the wall dividing Jerusalem. The next day, Israeli forces massed to the west. Two major battles ensued, one on Ammunition Hill, a vantage point to the north of the city walls, and the other by the Rockefeller Museum, a fortress-like building which overlooks the city wall from the northeast. When the Rockefeller fell, Israeli paratroopers led by Colonel Mordechai "Motta" Gur attacked the Old City at St. Stephen's Gate (commonly known as Lions Gate). By mid-morning of June 7, the Gate was under their control. The units then pushed through the alleys of the Via Dolorosa from the St. Stephen's Gate flank and swarmed over the Temple Mount on the other flank, toward the Western Wall.

The paratroopers could have proceeded west across the Old City, towards the Christian and Armenian Quarters. Or they could have stopped to deal with resistance in the Muslim Quarter. Instead, almost as if pulled by a magnet, they turned south towards the Western Wall at the bottom of the Jewish Quarter.

For nineteen years that Wall and the small open area in front of it had stood deserted. Only the occasional Jew with a diplomatic passport had managed to come through Jordan and visit the place.

Israeli soldiers were also fighting in the far southeast of their country at Suez and in the far northeast on the Heights of Golan, by the Sea of Galilee. Many were carrying transistor radios, and the word that the Old City had been taken travelled like wildfire. Soon, everyone who could was listening to the reporter on the Voice of Israel as he accompanied the soldiers fighting their way step by step to the Wall.

Those soldiers represented a cross-section of Israeli society. Among them were the religious and the secular, the Orthodox and the anti-religious. Regardless of background, they seemed to be in a trance of excitement and obsessed with a sense of mission.

Within an hour, the soldiers had reached the Wall. The words of the announcer moved a nation: "I cannot believe it. Here it is, I am seeing the Wall. The great stones. Everyone around me is touching the Wall. They are crying. I'm crying myself."

Within forty-eight hours, Jerusalem had become a unified city. Bulldozers moved in and razed the concrete walls that had divided it. They also razed the Mughrabi Quarter that had surrounded the Western Wall, creating a large open space in front of it. To this day it is not clear who ordered the bulldozers in. Hundreds of thousands of people streamed into the place that previously could accommodate only hundreds. But the great space torn out by the bulldozers was not beautiful. Its shape was the accidental result of where the bulldozers happened to stop.

Five years later, in 1972, I was designing Block 38 of the Jewish Quarter. My work there had been hampered because the space created by the bulldozers in 1967 had not been touched since. Yehuda Tamir, chairman of the Company for the Reconstruction and Development of the Jewish Quarter, and others realized that one could not design the edge of Block 38, which overlooks the Wall, without knowing how the space itself would be developed.

Then one day I answered the door to my office to find outside, in the dazzling sun of a Jerusalem noon, a grizzled red-bearded man who looked like a Klondike prospector. He introduced himself as Meir Ben-Dov, the archaeologist who, together with Benjamin Mazar, was in charge of the excavations around the southwest corner

of the Temple Mount. He wanted me to help him develop a plan for the excavated areas.

Teddy Kollek had been approached by Tamir with the suggestion that his group along with the Municipality and the Ministry of Religious Affairs (the authorities responsible for the praying area in front of the Wall) should jointly commission me to prepare a master plan for the area.

The proposition, needless to say, was overwhelming. Here I was being asked to propose a design for what is the holiest active place for Jews — the Temple Mount being inactive.

The Wall had been part of my life ever since childhood. My first visit to the Wall was before 1948. It was then invisible from anywhere in the city until one stood immediately in front of it. The Mughrabi Quarter, a large block of houses built in the fourteenth century in what was the Valley of the Cheesemakers, blocked it from sight.

I remember walking through the Jaffa Gate and on down David Street market, past the busy stalls, turning right through a narrower alley, always coming down steps, always descending, passing narrow passages that often sheltered beggars, and then all of a sudden, quite unexpectedly, there was the Western Wall, twenty feet away.

The space in front of it was like an unroofed outdoor room, about 30 metres long and 5 metres wide, bounded on one side by houses and on the other by the Wall itself. You had to tilt your head right back to see the top of the Wall. When you stood so close to it, the enormous size and presence of the stones, almost a metre high and four metres long, some weighing 5 tons, some 100 tons, were overwhelming.

The first five courses of the Wall were enormous stones of Herod's retaining walls. Above them were the rather large stones of the Umayyad period, laid when the damaged wall was repaired to accommodate the two mosques, al-Aksa and the Dome of the Rock, on the Temple Mount. Higher still were smaller stones laid through the initiative of Moses Montefiore, who on his visit to Jerusalem at the end of the nineteenth century was dismayed at the state of disrepair of the Wall.

In the joints between the stones, between these layers of history, protruded stubborn plants, green all year, flowering purple and white in summer. As a child, I wondered where they found the water and nourishment to survive.

The Jews began praying at the Wall sometime after A.D. 70, when Titus destroyed the Second (and last) Temple. The Wall replaced the Temple, which was off limits to Jews. At the ramp leading today to the Temple Mount, or as the Muslims call it the Haram esh-Sharif, there is a sign in several languages, put up by the chief rabbinate, forbidding Jews to enter the grounds of the Temple Mount. One may enter the Temple only when one is pure. In the past one purified oneself with the ashes of the red cow. As red cows have disappeared, with them went the means of purification. Only the High Priest may enter the Holy of Holies (the specific location of the chamber housing the tabernacle) and only on Yom Kippur.

The exact location of the Holy of Holies is also uncertain, so the entire area of the Temple Mount is out of bounds to Orthodox Jews, to eliminate the possibility of an unpure person going near it. Jews pray at the Wall because it is all that is left to them of the Temple. The Wall has become the holiest place for Jews, Orthodox or not — a remnant of the truly holy Temple itself, where the presence of God was believed to reside.

On my return to Israel in 1967, the Kotel, as the Western Wall is known in Hebrew (an abbreviation of Hakotel Ha Ma'aravi), had already been transformed by the bulldozers. Instead of appearing suddenly twenty feet away, the Wall was now visible as soon as I walked through Dung Gate. It could be seen from the Upper City or the Jewish Quarter. It seemed smaller, its great size overwhelmed by the large expanse in front of it — a space bigger than the Piazza San Marco, much bigger than Times Square.

Being given the responsibility for redesigning the space was overwhelming. This was not Mamilla, a new secular center for Jerusalem. This was not a housing development. It was the equivalent of being asked to redesign St. Peter's Square at the Vatican or the courtyard of the Great Mosque at Mecca. Except, as I had to remind myself constantly, the Wall was a place of anticipation. It is not a replacement for the Temple. It is the place where we remember the Temple and anticipate its rebuilding.

I asked myself how I felt about praying at the Wall. In the dogmatic judgement of the Orthodox, I would not be considered a religious person, but I do, nevertheless, consider myself to be religious, and my cultural and emotional roots in Judaism are deep. Many Israelis are like me: perhaps three-quarters of the people do not practice their religion in the conventional sense, though half may go to synagogue two or three times a year. The other quarter go at least every Saturday, some of them every day, some three times a day. As Saul Bellow noted when he visited Jerusalem, "There are many Israelis who do not believe, but there are few who have no religious life."

The Wall is obviously much more than a place where Orthodox Jews worship. Within a week of its liberation, nearly everybody in the country came there to pray, to meditate, or just to be there. The Wall's meaning clearly extends beyond religion: it is the symbol of Judaism in every one of its facets — as a nation, a religion, a people, a culture.

I began to explore the Wall, trying to understand its history. Meir Ben-Dov took me step by step, layer by layer, through the excavations.

The upper layer consisted of recent domestic buildings from the Ottoman period, then farther down a touch here and there of Mameluke structures, then the easily recognizable Crusader vaults and arches. As we descended farther we came to the enormous walls of the three Umayyad palaces, which had been built around the Temple Mount by the same dynasty that built the two great Muslim structures, al-Aksa and Dome of the Rock, in the seventh and eighth centuries soon after the death of Muhammad.

I was confused when I first saw the great walls of the three palaces, each of which was rectangular in shape with a central court. I thought they must be Herodian structures because I recognized the enormous framed stones of Herodian construction. But I learned that these were stones pilfered by the Umayyads from the Temple compound walls, after they had been toppled by Titus and his army during their destruction of the Temple in A.D. 70. It was amazing to see columns of marble and granite from the Second Temple laid down horizontally as foundations for the Umayyad palaces.

Yet farther down, we penetrated the remains of the water and sewer network of the Umayyads. Then there were Byzantine houses and bathhouses, the marble edging still around the baths, the carefully laid mosaic floors still intact. Below the Byzantine layer, we at last reached the Herodian street level. The enormous paving stones down there looked as if they had been laid only a few weeks ago. They were in perfect condition, with thin slots between them to allow the water to drain in what appeared to be a magnificently engineered network for water distribution. Ben-Dov's archaeologists have left some of the enormous dressed stones of Herod's walls lying at odd angles, just as they landed when they were toppled by Titus's soldiers from eighty feet above. The Byzantine builders must have simply dumped earth and rubble on top of them to get a flat surface for new buildings.

At first it is difficult to comprehend how these layers of construction could accumulate and build up to thicknesses as great as thirty feet. Essentially what has happened in Jerusalem, and I suppose in similar cities, is that the cycles of building, war, destruction, and rebuilding have raised the general level of the city about half a metre every century. The ruins were rarely cleared down to the original level. New construction was simply built on top of the old.

Later Ben-Dov guided me around to the northern end of the Western Wall. Under what is known as Wilson's Arch (the great bridge that connected the Upper City with Herod's Temple) the British archaeologist Charles Warren had dug a shaft beside the Wall down to the Herodian street level. As he dug, he exposed twelve more courses of perfect Herodian stone and then continued digging all the way down to bedrock, revealing several more courses. Some of them had been four, five or six layers below street level, but were made of dressed stone. I asked why the stones below street level had been dressed or, that is, smoothed. Ben-Dov explained, half-seriously, that the contractor was probably corrupt: paid by the piece, with a higher price for dressed stone than rough stone, he may have tried to maximize his profit by using more dressed stones than strictly necessary.

I also explored the history of the wall by rereading Josephus's *The Jewish War* (written in A.D. 75–79). It was one thing to read Josephus in my youth in Haifa and quite another to reread him while sitting on my terrace in the Old City, overlooking the Temple Mount, and to follow his hour-by-hour description of the great rebellion and the ensuing war.

I was particularly fascinated by his account of the great siege leading to the fall of the city to Titus. The city, Josephus tells us, had three walls. The outer wall was known as the Third Wall. It extended north from Jaffa Gate to enclose a considerable settlement in the northern part of the city. The two inner walls were called the Second and First Walls. The First Wall ran west from the Temple to today's Jaffa Gate, passing, in other words, within view of my terrace. The Romans first broke through the Third and Second Walls and then besieged the rest of the city. Attempting to overrun the Antonia Fortress and the Temple itself, they built ramps, poured hot oil, and shot balistae. It all happened just a few yards away from my terrace. I would sit there, almost hypnotized, imagining the sounds, the smells, the action — looking down from my terrace at the places where it all happened.

After a two-month siege, the First Wall too was overcome, and then came the destruction of all three walls and the burning of the Temple. Had I been there two thousand years earlier, I would have had a front row seat to this tragic event.

From my visit to Ben-Dov's excavations and my reading of Josephus, I became fascinated with Herod the Great. He was undoubtedly one of the great builders of all time. Those enormous stones of the Temple Mount fit so perfectly together that you can't slide a penny between them. One of the traditions at the Wall is to

109

write your wish or prayer down on a tiny piece of paper and slip it between the stones. But if you look closely, you see that most of the pieces of paper have been placed where the stone has eroded. Where the stone is sound, a piece of paper can hardly fit between the joints. I know that I can't get joints thinner than a half-centimetre from stone-masons today, yet here are slabs weighing many, many tons, not plastered but clean stone construction, extending hundreds of feet, and they are still firmly based on their foundations. Each course is absolutely even, about a metre high. The courses were predetermined and the stone was used only if it could be dressed to fit the exact dimensions of the course. Before the stones were placed, they were framed: slightly recessed, each stone was 3.5 and 7 inches in from each edge — another sign of Herod's extraordinary attention to detail.

The whole notion of building this enormous retaining wall round the little hill of Solomon's Temple in order to create a platform large enough to accommodate the Second Temple shows the grandeur of Herod's conception. The Wall runs a thousand feet in one direction and somewhat more in the other, so it is slightly more than five thousand feet long. Herod's Temple filled only about a quarter of the platform set on top of the walls.

The Temple building itself is said to have been completely covered with gold leaf so that when hit by the sun, it was almost blinding. There was a great gateway that led to the sanctuary, which contained the Holy of Holies. The magnificent retaining wall was crowned by an arcade of pilasters with capitals running all the way around the Temple Mount. Since Herod's architects were probably

Roman or Roman-trained, the Temple was built in the vocabulary of Roman or Greco-Roman architecture, with columns, capitals, and architraves.

Herod also created the palace of Herodion near Bethlehem, as well as the palace and fortress of Masada overlooking the Dead Sea, the aqueduct system leading to Jericho and the adjacent winter palaces, the city of Caesarea, and the three great towers at the western edge of Jerusalem. But Herod is known for his cruelty rather than his architectural genius. He was the evil Edomite who seized the crown and cooperated with the Romans. Stories prevail about Herod's cruelty and paranoia. This Herod the Great (73 B.C.–4 B.C.), hated by the Jews, is not Herod Antipas (21 B.C.–39 A.D.), who reigned at the time of the crucifixion of Jesus, but his father.

The search for an understanding of Herod took me again and again to the Wadi Kelt where Herod's aqueducts still bring water to Jericho, to his Herodion palace near Bethlehem and to the famous, or infamous, Masada, about 94 kilometres southeast of Jerusalem.

To many visitors, Masada brings to mind the last stand and mass suicide of Eleazar Ben Yair and his fanatical band, the final remnant of the failed rebellion of the Jews against the Romans. But it is also the site that Herod chose for a spectacular palace. The enormous cliff of Masada rises out of the desert and overlooks the Dead Sea. When you walk on its first platform hundreds of feet above the desert, you can see the ruins of the palace, the bathhouse, and the pool, as well as the cave where the patriots killed themselves. But if one fills in the missing walls, roofs, water, and vegetation, one realizes what an oasis this must have been. In the middle of that parched desert, all brown and yellow, the palace must have seemed the re-creation of Paradise. What an experience it must have been to drive by chariot for two days through the terrible Judean desert and arrive at Masada to find these hanging gardens and sparkling pools of water.

The palace of Herodion was just the opposite concept to Masada architecturally. Herod built a hill — "the shape of a woman's breast," Josephus tells us — and sank a palace in the middle of it. From afar, all you see is the hill; you have no idea that it contains any building at all. You climb a spiral road and discover, as if in the mouth of a volcano, a complete palace that looks out through little slits over the surrounding countryside.

111

Josephus writes in some detail about the amphitheatres, bath-houses, and temples that Herod built around the Mediterranean basin, in Damascus, Tyre, Beirut, and the Aegean islands. All this building, according to Dr. Robert Bull, who has been excavating Caesarea for many years, was part of a great international promotion campaign to encourage those port and trading cities to use his greatest enterprise of all, the port of Caesarea.

One of the greatest harbours of its time in the Mediterranean, equal to the harbour at Athens, Caesarea was built in a place that had no natural shelter or bay. All the jetties needed for protection were man-made. Herod began Caesarea from scratch, unencumbered by any previous construction. His goal was to build a great port that would attract all the trade from the Far East, coming through the Greek cities of Trans-Jordan, on through the Samarian mountains by Nablus to Caesarea for distribution to the Roman world. He developed the agriculture of spices and perfumes in the Valley of Jericho with his great irrigation program and it too was channelled through Caesarea, which partly explains how he financed these almost unbelievable construction programs. The recent excavations in Caesarea have uncovered over twenty enormous warehouses, each five metres wide and high and thirty-two metres long, in which goods were stored for shipment.

Caesarea had the world's first self-flushing sewer system. A jetty built out into the Mediterranean captured the prevailing current, flowing northward, and forced it into a channel that ran in a semi-circle behind the town and then returned through the sewers built under the streets, flushing the entire system into the sea.

To supply Caesarea with fresh water, Herod built an aqueduct sixteen kilometres long. Eight kilometres were above ground and the next eight kilometres were carved through the foothills east of Mount Carmel. Every one hundred and fifty feet, air shafts were drilled down through the mountain to provide oxygen to those digging the tunnel. An aqueduct must have a constant slope. It cannot be too steep or the water will move too fast, and if the slope is reversed, the water won't flow at all. Because the difference in level between Caesarea and the water source sixteen kilometres away was so small, the slope had to be computed carefully and the aqueduct built very exactly. Considering the technical means available at the time we have absolutely no idea how they achieved such finite accuracy.

At the source, an underground reservoir was constructed and many springs and wadis (watercourses) were tapped. The water channels were covered so that they would not be visible and vulnerable to an enemy.

The Cardo Maximus, the main street in Caesarea, was larger and even more magnificent than the one excavated in Jerusalem. Dr. Bull has recently uncovered the columns and bases of this cardo, which extends from the theatre all the way to the later Crusader castle.

Robert Bull believes Herod hired the best architects of his time, Roman, Greek, or local. We may not know who Herod's architects were, but I am convinced that Herod himself was actively involved in the design of his buildings. I don't say this on the basis of historical fact, but from observation of his works. There is a constant hand in them — themes recur and there is evident a great sensitivity to seizing the opportunities of a site. The designs of the palaces of Masada and Herodion, the scale and boldness of his structures, convince me that Herod was an imaginative and active participant in the design process.

There is a character to his work that differentiates it from the work of his Roman contemporaries. In part, the difference was technical: the Roman buildings of that time were mostly built out of rough brick, stone and mortar mix, which was then plastered and decorated, whereas Herod's work was finished cut stone, rarely used by the Romans. The explanation Ben-Dov gives is that to make plaster one must burn limestone, for which wood, never in abundance in the eastern Mediterranean, is needed. For his massive construction program Herod simply couldn't get enough plaster. He therefore resorted to what we recognize to be infinitely superior construction, which has lasted much longer, working the stone to the point where it is the actual finish, using no plaster at all.

Few builders of any age could compare with Herod the Great, and he is certainly the equal of any of the great Roman emperors. Just as Vivaldi was totally neglected throughout the nineteenth century and then came back to life in the twentieth century, and as Mendelssohn helped to revive Bach, who was equally unappreciated throughout the eighteenth and first half of the nineteenth centuries, the time has come to resurrect Herod, the great builder.

CHAPTER 10

LIFE CYCLES AT THE WESTERN WALL

Jerusalem was a minor Jebusite city before David conquered it and made it his capital. His son, King Solomon, expanded the city and built a temple, utilizing Phoenician craftsmen, materials and designers.

I am often asked, "What are the elements of Jewish architecture?" and "Where might one look for inspiration in designing Jewish institutions that have a link to their heritage?" Well, Solomon is not a good place to look because the People of the Book farmed out their design work to others. Several generations after Solomon's reign, the Temple was destroyed — and the first exile came at the hands of the Assyrians. In 538 B.C. Emperor Cyrus of Persia allowed the Jews to return and to build the Second Temple. By the time of Herod, following the Hashmona'im dynasty, Jerusalem was a glorious city, with the Second Temple rebuilt and expanded (only to be totally destroyed by the Roman Emperor Titus in A.D. 70). It was several generations after Titus's reign that the city was rebuilt, this time by Hadrian as Aelia Capitolina, a Roman city forbidden to

Jews. Then as Christianity emerged in the later part of the Roman era, Jerusalem became a Christian center. The Moslem conquest followed in A.D. 637, but the city was returned to Christianity by the Crusaders in the eleventh century. In A.D. 1187 the Moslems recaptured Jerusalem and remained in control through the Ottoman Empire until the British under Allenby took the city at the end of World War I.

Thinking about Herod and other aspects of Jerusalem's history led me to the eternal question Why Jerusalem? Two great world religions originated here; a third, Islam, has strong roots. Why on this spot — a city without a port, without a river, without any visible redeeming feature, a minor water source, on a watershed? Why not Damascus? Or Alexandria? Why not a city on the coast? Why at the edge of the desert? Part of the reason, I think, is that Jerusalem is in the geographic center of the land of Israel, or Palestine, which lies between the Jordan and the Mediterranean; and that land has been the tramping ground of almost every civilization that existed in the region. None of these civilizations could connect with its neighbors, either as conquerors or as traders, without passing through this territory. As the Egyptians traded with, or fought, the Mesopotamians, the Persians, and the Greeks, they had to travel through Palestine. When Alexander marched into the east, it was through Palestine. As the Romans expanded and established their Empire, they could not avoid Palestine. And then, almost through the energy set up by these events, wave followed wave — the Crusaders searching for the birthplace of Christ, the Ottomans extending their reach, and Napoleon looking for the antiquities of Egypt and Jerusalem.

Every time two cultures collide, something new and rich emerges, as Alexander's sojourn in Persia produced the wonderful heritage of Hellenistic culture. We think of these as rare events. But in Jerusalem there has been a constant grafting of one culture onto another, to produce this strange and magnificent organism, whose heart is the Temple Mount with the Wall forming the base around it.

To develop a plan for the new open space at the Western Wall, I needed to understand how that place was being used. I spent many hours observing the cycles of life at the Wall.

About this time (1973), I was asked to collaborate with the National Film Board of Canada in making a film about Jerusalem.

116

One of the things they were interested in capturing was the life at the Wall, and so I guided them through the events that took place there in the course of a week.

First, I took them down on a Monday morning — the day (with Thursday) of the bar mitzvah, when families come with their thirteen year old sons to celebrate their entry into manhood.

The entire piazza was covered with clusters of families, twenty or thirty people in each group. Most, clearly, were of Middle Eastern origin. Each bar mitzvah boy was dressed in white and wore the talith, a special shawl. He was carried on the shoulders of the men in the family as they walked across the square in front of the Wall. At the fence which divides the secular from the holy area (another at right angles divides men from women) the men and the boy went on without the women. As soon as the boy entered the praying area, the older women, grandmothers and aunts, dressed traditionally with veils over their heads, began to cry out the high-pitched North African ululation which marks both festive and sad events in their lives.

The NFB cameraman didn't know where to focus. There were about fifteen or twenty bar mitzvahs going on at the same time in different parts of the piazza, yet each group seemed to feel as if they were the only ones there.

After the prayers, the families moved on to sit on the stones or low walls and eat their picnics. A few hundred feet away one could smell some of the delicacies that were being cooked.

That night I took the film crew out to the Wall again. The place was completely silent. Though the night was dark and moonless, the entire piazza, the Wall, and the buildings surrounding it were lit by dozens of floodlights. A few dark figures, bowing repeatedly, moved forward and sideways. They were Hasidim dressed in black with fur hats, passionately praying. To one side was a man in modern clothes, clutching the stones, his head pressed against them, motionless. On the other side, across the fence, in the women's area, three women were standing at the Wall barely moving. Suddenly the silence was interrupted. Three hundred yards away near the security fence, three or four long Mercedes taxis came to a stop. Dozens of men, dressed in black with black hats and with black sideburns, rushed out like a swarm of bees and headed for the Wall. In their midst was an older man with white hair and a white beard, perhaps their rabbi. The

117

students around him scurried to the Wall and their high-pitched sounds of prayer and song erupted in the silent Jerusalem night. The presence of the film crew did not seem to disturb them and after half an hour of loud prayer they departed, walking backwards, keeping their faces toward the Wall. Only when they were about a hundred yards away from it did they turn around and scuttle back into the waiting taxis.

On Thursday night I invited the film crew to my own house. We sat on the terrace, cameras set up. I did not tell them what to expect. As the sun set, a group of soldiers appeared carrying a large platform, a kind of stage, and then arranged rows of what appeared to be small aluminum cans in front of the piazza.

Something that looked like a large net was stretched across the eastern end of the square. Somebody tested the public address system. Then through Dung Gate came ranks of marching soldiers, wearing the red berets of the elite paratroopers. They were arriving for swearing-in ceremonies at the end of their three-month intensive training program.

Their families followed them and clustered round the edges of the area marked by the aluminum cans. A soldier walked around igniting the aluminum cans — they were torches — and, as they were lit, the floodlights on the Wall were dimmed. One by one the soldiers shouted their oath of allegiance, then went up to the stage to receive a Bible. After a short speech by their commander, the net stretched at the east end of the piazza was ignited and it blazed with the emblem of the paratroopers — a giant parachute with wings. Almost thirty feet long, it was bright enough to light the whole Wall.

On the Friday evening, the eve of the Sabbath, the piazza was transformed once more. People started arriving well before sunset, when the praying began. Thousands came, including groups of black-robed Hasidim and multicoloured clusters of tourists. Then the yeshiva students came marching from the southern side of the piazza, across the piazza in rows of six, arms entwined, wearing white shirts and white skullcaps, singing for the arrival of Shabbat and dancing to the rhythm of their song, their pale faces matching their white clothes.

As the students moved into the praying area itself, they formed a circle and continued their song and dance. The tourists gathered around them, some clapping hands to the rhythm. But the Hasidic Jews continued their meditative prayer as if nothing had happened.

On the women's side, the older women were close to the Wall, their heads covered. Their bare-headed young daughters stood nearby in brightly colourful Shabbat dress.

Some events cannot be observed in the weekly cycle of the life of the Wall. They are annual events of great import. Jerusalem is the city of three annual pilgrimages: Passover, Shavuot and Sukkot. On each of these holidays, as well as on the New Year and Yom Kippur, tens of thousands come to pray at the Wall. Perhaps the most moving are the events of the ninth day of the month of Av. This is the anniversary of the destruction of both Solomon's First and Second Temples. On this day of fasting more than a hundred thousand people come to the Wall. From my house, I can see that the entire piazza from the Wall all the way to Dung Gate is covered with humanity. I saw a similar concentration of people on a day in which a demonstration was called to protest the detention of Russian Jews in the Soviet Union.

This invaluable period of observation and study brought me to realize that the Western Wall was a place of both intimate meditation and national assembly. But more than that, it was a place of contrasts and contradictions.

CHAPTER 11

THE FIRST DESIGN

As I thought more about the task of designing the space in front of the Western Wall, I realized there would be the standard urban design questions as well as the specific questions posed by the unique and sacred nature of the site. The entrances to the piazza, one from the David Street market through an alley, one from Dung Gate, a third from the stairs built next to Porat Yosef, were all casually constructed, not carefully considered. The plan somehow had to provide for connections between the Wall and the city, like arteries extending from the heart into the body.

As I walked in the piazza I noticed that many people passed by the Wall without any interest in it. Arabs from the adjacent village of Silwan came through Dung Gate and walked past the Wall on their way to the markets, as did Arab children going to schools in the Old City. There was no separation between the sacred and the profane, no screen, edge, or line to make you feel you were either in a holy place or passing by and looking into it. It seemed to me that it was important to articulate that kind of distinction.

Another critical question concerned the structures that would define the western edge of the space, the edge opposite the Wall. I was working with Tamir and the Company on Block 38 in the Jewish

Quarter at that time, but we had yet to define what type of building belonged there. There was common agreement, however, that the edge of Block 38 should not be built up with residences. The Wall and the space in front of it warranted institutions of the highest symbolic significance (legal, religious, or governmental) and no one should have his living room or bathroom directly overlooking the Wall. A couple of older buildings survived on the cliff immediately across from the Wall, and there was the new yeshiva to the north, but new buildings would have to be erected to define what was at that point a ragged edge.

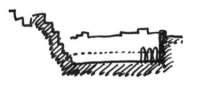

And so began my search. For several weeks I explored, sketched, and discarded. Out of the many ideas and thoughts, one took root. The accumulated rubble and debris of two thousand years was hiding twelve buried courses of the Wall of the Second Temple; it had to go. Exposing the full magnificence of Herod's Wall to view would almost double the height of the Wall and restore the sense of grandeur that I well remembered from my visits as a child.

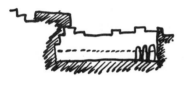

Digging thirty feet down, we would also increase the difference in height between the praying area and the Jewish Quarter. A height difference of no more than six storeys would become one of nine storeys. But the most important reason for excavating the rubble was that it would allow prayers to be said on the very street built at the time of the Second Temple.

I kept drawing a cross-section showing the towering Wall, the Herodian street as the praying area, and the long rise to the edge of the Jewish Quarter. I was left with the problem of the nine storey cliff. No matter what design approach I used, the new building edge on the opposite side invariably competed with and overwhelmed the Wall.

I compared this space with every public space I knew — St. Peter's Square, Piazza San Marco, Piazza Navona, Piazza del Campo in Siena, the great Maidan in Esfahan. I compared their dimensions, heights, proportions. As I made these comparisons, I invariably started to recognize the differences. In the European piazza there is usually a focal point: the colonnade of St. Peter's focuses on the domed church, as does the one at St. Mark's in Venice. But in the piazza of the Western Wall, there was no focal point, just that enormous mass of wall, the place of anticipation.

I also saw that none of those piazzas and squares, not even the smaller ones, were hospitable to intimate worship and meditation. There is no niche or corner anywhere in the Piazza San Marco or St. Peter's where one can feel alone with one's God. They are spaces designed for the grand assembly; intimacy can be found inside the churches perhaps. But I had to find a way to create a space so that a worshipper next to the Wall did not feel like a speck of sand in a wilderness. The usual grand piazza contradicted the whole notion of meditative praying.

Often in tackling a problem in architecture or urban design, one resorts to familiar models for guidance and inspiration. As Ecclesiastes wrote, "What was, shall be . . . There is nothing new under the sun." But there are also times when resorting to the familiar becomes an impediment. It is often at those moments when an architect makes his most exciting discoveries.

So it was with the piazza. It was, after all, a public space, a square. In the traditional model the public space is always defined by the buildings around it. The shapes, heights, proportions of the buildings might vary, but there are always buildings to establish the boundaries. Slowly, I began to question the basic premise of a piazza and to seek alternatives. Only the Wall should form an edge to the great space. For the opposite side, at first the formulation was vague: a non-building edge, an amorphous edge, a disappearing edge, were the ways in which I expressed it to myself as I tried to create a counterpoint to the Wall. I had a similar fixation about the space itself. I was forever drawing a flat piazza. Sometimes I would gently slope it, as in Sienna, but for months I could not escape from the obvious notion of a single flat space.

One day David Zifroni, the deputy director of the Company for the Reconstruction and Development of the Jewish Quarter, walked into my office as I was doodling away. He looked over my shoulder — we had known each other for many years — and asked what I was doing. I explained to him the dilemma: the great Wall to the east; the Herodian street with the Jewish Quarter nine storeys above it to the west; a flat piazza in between; a series of unsuccessful sketches in which I had tried to design the western edge in a manner sympathetic to the Wall across the piazza. "What you ought to do," he said, "is think of yourself as Herod's architect." And he went on about his business.

If I were Herod's architect, what would I do? If I had a street a hundred feet below the edge of the Jewish Quarter, "the Upper City," and I had to connect them . . . it became clear suddenly — I would follow the bedrock! I would simply step up, layer by layer, from street level to the upper city, creating terraces that would follow the natural slope of the rock. At that moment I knew that this was not a piazza at all; it could not be and should not be a piazza. It was a series of spaces that ascended from the lower level of two thousand years ago and followed the natural topography of the land. Instead of a nine storey edge that would compete with the Wall, a sequence of terraces would rise gradually, never forming a firm edge between the piazza and the buildings of the Jewish Quarter. I drew up the design, we made models and cross-sections, and everything seemed to fall into place, every issue that had worried me seemed to be resolved.

The lowest terrace would be only thirteen metres wide, just the width of the Herodian street. A few people gathering for prayers there would feel as if they were in their own intimate area, not in a vast space. The next terrace, two metres higher, would overlook this area, and the next would be higher again by another couple of metres. The bigger the event, the larger the crowd at the Wall, the more terraces would be in use. This arrangement resolved another dilemma of the single piazza concept: if there were a hundred thousand people, most would feel themselves to be too far away from the Wall. With the terracing, each level of worshippers would look out over those below, and, even as the terraces filled up, each worshipper would always feel a connection with the Wall.

Now I turned to resolving the connections to the surrounding city. With the whole space ascending in terraces it was easy to weave in a set of stairways, rising gradually. I developed seven different ways of getting into the piazza — the original three entrances and four new ones. Even the design of the institutions that formed the western edge of the space seemed to resolve itself. Rather than being arrogant buildings proclaiming their own importance across from the Wall, they would be the most modest of buildings, almost like landscape; they would be amorphous, terracing softly westward, bowing to the Wall as the only massive element in the place.

The reconciliation of archaeology and new construction was also resolved. We knew that as we excavated down to the Herodian street level we would find some important archaeological remains. We made an agreement, with the Mayor, the archaeologists, and the religious groups, that anything found within thirteen metres of the Wall (the width of the street) would be removed, whatever it was: the street was to become the new praying area. But what if we found some important remains farther back? The terraced formation made it easy. They could be integrated into the terraces, or preserved under them without disrupting the sequence of public space.

What about casual passing traffic? An arcaded street connecting Dung Gate with the Old City markets could be tucked under one of the terraces, creating a bypass which would separate the sacred and the secular. An archaeological discovery a few months later proved how right this solution was. At the time there were gaps in our knowledge of what existed underground in the western end of the precinct. One day, under a building we were restoring next to the David Street market, the archaeologists found another older market, two storeys below, running perpendicular to David Street and parallel to the Wall. It joined up with El Wad Road, a street leading to Damascus Gate, one of the two principal Roman Cardos. Amazingly, it came out in the piazza just in line with the arcaded street I'd proposed. In other words, our new arcaded street, tucked under terraces, and the old street we had now discovered would form a continuous line right across the Old City from Dung Gate to Damascus Gate. And as if that was not enough, four months later, when excavating outside Dung Gate, the archaeologists again hit the pavement of the Roman Cardo. (This was not the Roman Cardo we discovered in the Street of the Jews, but a secondary one following the lower section of the city.) Without knowing it I had proposed an arcaded street that turned out to be right in line with the Roman Cardo, plugging into a surviving section of it at one end and reaching the archaeological remnants of it at the other.

Once the plan of the precincts was drawn, I made another sketch that extended the terracing southward into the archaeological gardens to the south of the Wall. By simply extending the terracing towards the southeast, we would expose and integrate the remnants of every period in the history of the city. Naturally, the most recent periods would be on top: first, Ottoman; then, descending toward the south, Mameluke and Crusader, with the Umayyad palaces beneath them; then Byzantine and, farther down, Roman (Aelia Capitolina), Herod's Second Temple, and, even farther down, the First Temple.

I met Meir Ben-Dov, the archaeologist, and showed him the sketches. When he saw them, something seemed to click. He remembered a passage from Josephus that almost described my new plan.

He started wading through Josephus's *The Jewish War* until he found the passage. It said that on the western side of the Temple, the city ascended gradually like an amphitheatre toward the crown of the upper city. So it turned out that what I had evolved in my own plans for the Wall area was similar to Josephus's description of nearly two thousand years before.

Once I was clear about the organization of terraced piazzas I faced the fundamental quesion of the building vocabulary — that generating geometry that would help to unify the spaces and buildings. It might even enable several architects to design parts within the whole. This was the problem I struggled with in Manchat and in Mamilla, but here there was an added dimension. At the Wall, with its series of piazzas and buildings, there would be so many variables arising out of the nature of the site (archaeology, level changes not yet anticipated, etc.) that a strong framework was needed.

I thought about those elements which give a city unity and relate and connect buildings and spaces so that the whole is greater than the parts: a Georgian square, where many individual houses, each with its restrained, fenestrated facade, form a continuous wall containing the city square; the village, where the repetitive clustered agglomeration of the cubic volumes of houses, domes and vaults form a man-made hill; or the city grid from which such great cities as New York, Barcelona, Philadelphia, or Peking derive their particular building arrangements. It was this pattern of urban geometries — a macro-scale geometry that transcended individual buildings to form something more — that I was searching for. I wanted a sense of organization which would give order to the precinct in front of the Wall.

The grid analogy was revealing. Usually a grid implies equal divisions from top to bottom and side to side. But this site was extremely unbalanced, truly asymmetrical. On the Wall side the scale was enormous — the Wall itself and its great stones. On the other side, in the upper city, the scale was small, as in domestic Ottoman architecture, with six or eight metre blocks of houses with domes and vaults. It was difficult to see how a rigid grid could work as an organizing system. What was needed was a grid that transformed in scale like a piece of woven Scottish tartan. The problem of the transformation of scale, going from large to small without abrupt change, fascinated me.

I have been interested in the problem of transformation for years. I've always felt city planning could be seen as a problem of transformations of scale and that many urban designers fail because they don't recognize this. The modern city includes single family houses and skyscrapers, large buildings and small ones. In the traditional city there was less diversity of scale, and the different building types evolved over time without sudden disruptions. The larger structures — temples and palaces — were always appropriately set apart from the more delicate fabric of residential buildings. This sense of homogeneity prevailed in the nineteenth century city before the advent of the skyscraper.

In the contemporary city, two elements (large buildings and small buildings) are at play, but the city is also subject to continuous change and growth. Thus the added problem of transformation. A neighborhood of two storey townhouses is disrupted by twenty storey apartment buildings constructed following zoning changes. In an expanding downtown area, thirty storey office towers extend into zones of two storey factories. Small is juxtaposed against the large. The pattern is inorganic and frequently chaotic.

If there were an organic logic and order to the form of cities, the change in scale would be gradual. The city would develop in the general form of a pyramid, gradually becoming more dense and larger in scale. One need only examine downtown Houston to see the total antithesis: a cluster of thirty or forty skyscrapers, falling off abruptly into a no-man's land of parking lots and two storey buildings; and throughout Houston, like wild oats, rising out of a low-density sprawl are the unexpected protrusions of yet other towers.

The problems of transformations do not have much precedent in architecture. I was looking to music and painting to discover a framework that gradually transformed from large scale to small scale in a geometric progression. The Dutch artist M.C. Escher provided an inspiration. His work teaches lessons not only in transforming size but, what is even more complex and more difficult, transforming images. In Escher's drawings an isolated single detached house is gradually transformed into larger, more compact, and multilevel groupings. Nowhere can one draw a line and say, "This is where Type A ends and Type B starts."

In the case of the space in front of the Wall, I thought of starting with a grid of regular squares. The diagonal of a square is in the same proportion to its sides as the square root of two is to one. I took my first grid of regular squares, then rotated it through forty-five degrees, and used the diagonals of the first as the sides of the second grid, making larger squares: just twice the area, in fact. I went through the transformation again, and the squares of the third grid had sides twice the length of those on the first and four times the area. I established the first square in the series to be equal in size to the houses in the Jewish Quarter, a grid six metres on a side. Then transforming this upwards in size four times, I arrived at a twenty-four metre grid at the other end, quite appropriate to the monumental scale of the Wall.

What about the vertical plane? I wanted the flat public space of the praying levels to transform into the three-dimensional volumes of the buildings on the ridge in such a way that the entire area formed a continuous build-up. I didn't want a visible line separating the public piazza from the buildings. I sought interpenetration in both directions, with the public piazzas extending into the buildings and the volumes of the buildings extending into the piazzas.

My third objective, almost a byproduct of the first two, was to see if the institutional buildings could be designed almost like urban landscape or urban topography. Rather than being perceived as set on a site, the buildings should appear to rise in continuous layers, like a hill that has been terraced — the stone-terraced olive groves around Jerusalem or the terraces of rice paddies in the hills of

Western Wall —
The Western Wall and the piazza
in front of it as it is today.
Note the archaeological
excavations surrounding the
western and southern walls.
(Pantomap Israel Ltd.)

Western Wall — Details of the makeshift conditions by the Wall, 1975. The praying area has
been cleared and paved; the archaeological excavations continue to the west and south. The edge
of the Jewish Quarter is an accidental result of where the bulldozers stopped in 1967.
(Pantomap Israel Ltd.)

Western Wall — The Wall in the earlier part of the century.

Western Wall — Thousands gathering by the Wall for a demonstration of sympathy for Russian Jewry.

Soldiers praying at the Wall.

Western Wall — Presentation of the model of the Western Wall Precinct to the President of Israel, Ephraim Katzir, 1975. From left to right: M. Safdie, E. Katzir, unidentified, Mayor Teddy Kollek.

Western Wall — The first model of the Western Wall Precinct plan, 1974. Note the terraces ascending from the Wall, the arcaded passage, the small ante-room piazza by Dung Gate, the terraced public buildings to the west and Yeshivat Porat Yosef.

Western Wall — The revised new model of the Western Wall Precinct, 1982 (montage). Note the revised archaeological gardens, the integration of archaeology with terraces and the preservation of the old buildings on the cliff to the left. *(David Harris)*

Western Wall —
Excavation by the Wall showing
the perfect courses of Herodian construction.

Western Wall —
The Herodian street, nine meters below
the current surface, uncovered in perfect condition.

Western Wall — Detail of the revised model of the Western Wall Precinct. In the foreground are the gates to the Umayyad Palace and the partial reconstruction of the Herodian stair to the temple. To the left is the Dung Gate entrance piazza connecting to the arcaded street atop the Roman Cardo; to the upper left are the restored buildings on the cliff. *(Sam Sweezy)*

Western Wall — Looking south towards the praying areas placed atop the Herodian street. *(Sam Sweezy)*

People praying at the Wall. *(Sam Sweezy)*

Western Wall — The archeological gardens showing the section restoring the Umayyad Palace, reconstruction of its gateways and the courtyard surrounded by colonnades with its pools, canals and fruit trees. Porat Yosef is in the background. *(Sam Sweezy)*

Southeast Asia. If the buildings could become a kind of landscape, rich and complex though they were, their presence would nevertheless be minimized in comparison with the uncompromising mass of the Wall.

Once these objectives had become clear, translating them into an urban design plan was a joyful process. The geometric progression seemed to work perfectly as it transformed from Herod's scale to the domestic scale of the upper city. The largest grid for the public praying areas would weave into the archaeological gardens, where the walls and walkways of the Umayyad palaces and Herod's streets fit in perfectly. The next range would be the upper piazzas, which rose in steps of increasing height toward the upper city. As the scale changed again, it defined the arcaded street that was to be the bypass from Dung Gate to the markets. Then again it transformed to the scale of the public rooms and halls of the Rabbinical Supreme Court and the other institutions that were planned for the future and at last arrived at the scale of the houses I designed on the cliff of Block 38.

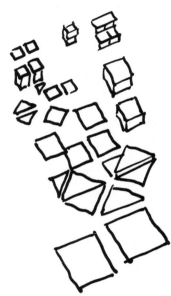

Time might well add other dimensions to these transformations. In the plan for the precinct of the Wall, the transforming grid is distinct, definite, uncompromising, but I know that variation from the grid will emerge in defiance of the imposed order. Out of the past, a layer of archaeology will come through almost like a dye through a fabric. In the future, buildings we can't envision now will be constructed in response to requirements and needs unknown today, giving yet another layer of richness.

But there is another level of experience which I have so far known only in music, and that is the richness and joy that come from the interaction of one grid pattern on another, as in a fugue. Bach takes a theme and repeats it in several layers, shifting the starting point, juxtaposing it, rotating it, and interpenetrating it with several instruments, so that it becomes increasingly rich and complex with layers of meaning. I have always wondered if the same possibilities exist in architecture and urban design — layers of transformed grids, each one constructed over previous geometries imprinted on the site and incorporating patterns of human activity and man-made forms built over the geological and topographical forms of the land.

What Bach did with the fugue, we must learn to do in architecture. When the making of urban space truly acknowledges the activities in the city with all their complexity and variety, the dividing line between natural and man-made will soften and disappear and we will no longer think of a landscape as one kind of pleasure and a town as another. This is not an empty speculation for which there is no precedent — it is reminiscent of something of the past: the indigenous village, which through a process akin to evolution in nature achieves a quality that makes it almost of "nature."

Between that achievement and our present situation is a period of great alienation between man and nature. Ahead of us is the prospect of a more complex, more intricate, and more harmonious relationship.

CHAPTER 12

TEDDY KOLLEK, GOLDA MEIR AND THE ECHELONS OF POWER

Usually when I am in Jerusalem, I sleep right through the pre-sunrise chanting of the muezzin. But one morning, I awoke early, charged up, slightly tense. It was an important day: I was to go with the Mayor to present the model for the Western Wall to Golda Meir, the Prime Minister.

I sat watching the sun rise over the Mount of Olives, between the Augusta Victoria spire and the Dome of the Ascension. The light kindled the hundreds of domes that form the skyline of the Old City, igniting them with bouncing light. Soon, at six-thirty, my housekeeper, Abdul el Hamid, arrived, bringing hot loaves of bread.

I had my favorite breakfast, which I have adopted from Ian Fleming's James Bond — Turkish coffee and fresh figs with yogurt. To this, I added some fresh sesame rolls and fresh juice squeezed from Jericho oranges. The coffee I flavored with cardamom.

The soft, pinkish light now gave way to the blinding glare that flooded from the east. I left the house, taking refuge from the sun in the still deeply shaded alleys. As I walked up the Street of the Chain, merchants were opening up their stalls, some hanging out their merchandise, others pausing for morning coffee and chatting before their day's work. "Sabah el Chair," they said — "Good morning." "Sabah el nur — a morning of light," I answered in traditional greeting. Beyond the crossroads of the Crusader butcher market were the vegetable and fruit stalls. Fellaheen women were arranging colourful turnips, tomatoes, cucumbers, radishes and figs in front, competing with the more established merchants within the vaulted halls behind. I continued to the clearing at the end of the market, the small square by the Citadel where I had parked my car. The blast of sunlight was blinding. I decided to drive my white convertible Beetle to City Hall even though it was barely 400 yards away.

I walked into City Hall where the familiar security men appeared. They were the antithesis of bodyguards one would expect in Jerusalem — two unarmed men near retirement.

"Shall we go in your car, or would you like a ride in an open convertible?" I asked Teddy.

"Let's go in yours," he replied cheerfully. It was symbolic of the open life of Jerusalem that its Mayor would proceed in an open convertible, unencumbered, to the Prime Minister's office.

We drove together westward through the neighborhood of Rehavia, down the Valley of the Cross and up onto the hill where the government compound is laid out, bypassing the Knesset (Israeli parliament), and continuing on to the three bureaucratic-looking slabs that house the government ministries. We pulled up to the last one — the office of the Prime Minister, Golda Meir.

The security guards recognized Teddy, making it easy for us to pass through the utilitarian outer offices. In the anteroom, we met Meir's personal secretary and were soon joined by the Minister of Justice, Ya'acov Shimshon Shapira, who was also Chairman of the Cabinet Committee for Jerusalem Affairs.

The presentation model of the Western Wall precinct we had made in Montreal had been sent ahead. As we were ushered in to the meeting room, next to the Prime Minister's private office, I saw the model set up on the centre table. The Prime Minister's suite of rooms had an understated simplicity about them. Each room was plain with some wood panelling, in all quite modest. Through the small windows I could see the Hebrew University's new campus and glimpses of the Israel Museum.

The Prime Minister entered and walked directly towards us. After the usual informal introductions, she immediately bent over and started squinting at the model. She alternately smiled and looked toward the Minister of Justice, the Mayor, and myself.

My eyes were fixed on Golda Meir's every move. I was impressed by her enormous, almost cylindrical legs. In spite of their great size, there was a distinct elegance about them — they met the ground like two great Doric pillars, symbolizing her political strength and personal determination. She inquired about the excavations: how long might it take to dig down to the Herodian street? What did we expect the reaction of the Orthodoxy to be? What did we know about the archaeology in the area? We had answers to some questions, speculations about others. Surprisingly, most of her questions had to do with the substance of the plan and not with the political issues surrounding its realization. But she realized that the plan must be carefully navigated through many political minefields.

I sensed she imagined herself walking through this reconstructed square. The twinkle in her eye was irresistible. She turned to the Minister of Justice and instructed him to bring the proposal to the attention of the Cabinet Committee for Jerusalem Affairs. At that moment I felt certain the model would soon be turned into reality.

Several months after the meeting, on October 6, 1973, the Yom Kippur War broke out. Unlike the wars before it, this war devastated the psyche of Israelis. It brought a sudden end to that spirit of euphoria, to the belief in Israel as a world power able to cope with every challenge — military, economic or otherwise.

The earlier 1967 war had transformed a country filled with self-doubt, recession, emigration and a sense of military insecurity into a victorious nation. From the perspective of time it is easy to see how passive and uncompromising Israeli leadership was towards negotiations for settlement between 1967 and 1973. The very idea of another war was shunted aside. This political posture reflected a more fundamental shift in attitudes of the population towards material wealth — the good life no longer being one modestly achieved through work and building and the making of a community. After 1967, Israel became truly westernized and increasingly absorbed the values and tastes of North America. There was something tragicomic

133

in hearing Israelis chat about what happened between Carrington and Krystal in "Dynasty." People stayed home on Fridays so as not to miss the next installment about J.R. in "Dallas." The national pastime had become the collection of stereos, videos and the latest contraptions of electronic magic.

In that sense, the 1973 war — surprising in its occurrence and dear in its cost of lives and resources — shocked the population into a reassessment. Every major project was now reassessed with skepticism, even on occasion with defeatism. And so it was for the Western Wall; the optimism of "all possible" now gave way to a "mostly impossible" attitude.

This mood obviously had its effects on a major project such as the Western Wall, but Teddy continued to push it. My plan was not the first for the area, and alternative schemes continued to surface. The Ministry of Religious Affairs had commissioned a plan some years back from the Japanese-American sculptor Isamu Noguchi, who had earlier designed the sculpture garden for the Israel Museum. Noguchi proposed to excavate (as I did) but he placed an enormous black block, a slightly tapered, round-edged cube perhaps sixty feet across, in the middle of the praying area. A platform at the present plaza level was to be built around the block, leaving part of the terrace below in shadow and the portion above in sunlight.

Another plan was developed by my former employer Louis Kahn. He had been commissioned to redesign the Hurva Synagogue and extended his plan to include a wide ceremonial passage from Hurva in the heart of the Jewish Quarter to a large arcade defining the western edge of the square opposite the Wall. Kahn did not propose to excavate the area in front of the Wall.

The design by Kahn was meaningful to me and perhaps addressed the same needs as the seven entrances in my plan, the idea of powerful connections to the city giving architectural form to the ceremony and ritual. But I thought Noguchi's plan was preposterous, reflecting a total misunderstanding of Judaism. His great black stone was a caricature of the Ka'aba in Mecca. Noguchi explained that it would commemorate the Holocaust, but to me the black rock was an inappropriate memorial to the Holocaust. Moreover such a memorial would dominate the precinct around the Wall.

In October of 1974, the Mayor asked me to present my plan to the Jerusalem Committee at a meeting attended by both Noguchi and

Kahn. The meeting took place at Mishkenot Sha'ananim, in Fisher Hall, a vaulted meeting room looking into the lush gardens of the Montefiore housing. I presented the plan with the model. Larry Halprin, Bruno Zevi, and other old friends were there, but my attention was focused on Kahn. All the complexities of the relationship between mentor and rebellious disciple were in full play. As an apprentice in Kahn's office I was a critical admirer, continually sorting out what I admired from what I rejected. When *Time* magazine called Kahn for comments on Habitat after its opening, he was reserved and mildly critical, questioning the enormous structural effort necessary. Kahn had his reservations not only about me but about many others who developed under his influence, including Robert Venturi and Tim Vreeland.

Kahn was clearly concentrating; his short figure stooped forward, his deeply scarred face (from a childhood burning) was glowing. His blue eyes were intense behind thick-framed glasses, which he had worn since a cataract operation. His straight white hair fell over his forehead in a boyish way. At seventy, he looked mischievously youthful and, in spite of the scars, easily lovable. Silence fell as I finished my presentation.

"You are too exuberant, Moshe," he said. "There is a nervous excitement about the forms. There are too many arches. You must seek calmness. You must understate. There is just too much going on."

Perhaps the model was too detailed. Perhaps I had made it too much architecture and too little urban design. I reflected further that the real problem with models is that we look down on them from above. Real buildings we see from ground level. I responded, "I know what you mean, Lou, but look down here, right by the Wall. The terraces are subdued, no arches are visible."

Noguchi rejected the plan unequivocally. Also in his seventies, he had high cheek bones over slightly sunken cheeks, freckled skin, very calm eyes, his bald head almost a perfect sphere. He stood up and walked towards the model with an air of oriental meditation. He did not mention his own plan or the fact that he had made one. He stood there, stating calmly but firmly, "I disagree with the plan. I do not think it catches the spirit of the place. I do not understand its attitude about worship."

As he spoke, I did not see him or the others in the room. I saw the image of his model — that great black block of his, rising through the platform in front of the Wall. He spoke of worship and I thought of his pagan altar. I felt my blood boiling. I wanted to scream out, "Your difficulty is in understanding the worship of a god who is not an object and needs no object by which to be represented. That plan of yours needs the physical representation of the god — to transform one's emotion through the contemplation of an object to the abstraction of the monotheistic being. You do not understand the fundamentals of Judaism!"

Of course, I did not say any of this. Instead, I calmly responded, "Well, Mr. Noguchi, as your own plan for the area indicates, we have a very different vision and understanding of what is appropriate."

Observers told me later they were appalled that Noguchi didn't qualify his comments by saying that he believed in his own plan and then go on to highlight the difference in the two approaches.

Another impediment to my Western Wall plan was the change in government shortly after the Yom Kippur War. Golda Meir resigned and was replaced as Prime Minister by Yitzhak Rabin. This meant a whole new round of submissions. I girded my loins, tried to feel optimistic, and waited for the new chapter to unfold.

TEDDY KOLLEK AT WORK

My work in Jerusalem has become inseparable from my relationship with Teddy Kollek. Whenever I arrive in the city, he is one of the first people I call. We get up to date on issues and matters that need attention and usually make a date for the following morning. Typically, I see him at 6 a.m. when he is fresh and alert.

His office is on the top floor of the modest city hall built during the British mandate. It is a simple, medium-sized room which looks out on the landscaped square of the Russian compound on one side and towards Mamilla on the other. His large desk is covered with papers and paraphernalia, the bookshelves behind him are packed with books, most personally dedicated to him. Framed first date issued postage stamps of Jerusalem hang on the walls alongside caricatures, many of him and the city. Easy chairs and a sofa occupy one corner, a meeting table the other. I always sit across from him at his desk. A few minutes go by as he finishes signing papers and giving final instructions to his secretary. I always come armed with lists so that in the intensity of the conversation nothing will be forgotten. This is how one meeting went:

Item one: Harvard business. Some of my students have worked on a plan for the Damascus Gate. I think it is a good one. There is some resistance by the transportation planners who are trying to pack more buses into it. What should we do?

"Get me Avi Sperber," he calls out to his secretary. By now it is 6:15 a.m. — Avi is obviously still at home.

"Avi, good morning. I hope I didn't wake you up?" he says, knowing well that he did. "I'm very concerned over the number of buses at the Damascus Gate. I was speaking to Safdie (he makes a sign for me to get on the little extension earphone attached to his own phone). Forty buses is impossible; we will never get approval for this. Let's be more modest about what we can accommodate there."

Avi explains, Teddy responds. The number of buses is settled: twenty-seven. I sit back in the chair.

Item two: "Teddy, about Mamilla — we're inviting proposals, so we need the District Committee's approval on the project. Because of their heavy agenda, they haven't been able to discuss it yet." I've hardly finished when he calls, "Get me Rafi" (Rafi Levy, the chairman of the District Planning Committee).

"Rafi, good morning." Rafi has obviously been up. "How are you? What happened with this affair of the land negotiation by the Greek Orthodox church — have we settled matters with them? Did you speak with the Archbishop? Thank you, I really appreciate it. I think you should let the Greek Orthodox Patriarch know what is going on. By the way, we have a problem with Mamilla: we want to start building the road. We need approval. We can't get on the agenda for a month. Rafi, do you think you could get it on this Tuesday — it's really important to begin this. You'll try? Thank you."

Item three: Porat Yosef. "We're still trying to settle the disagreements over the design with the rabbis, Teddy. I appreciate the letter you wrote to Stephen Shalom. He did too. We have his full backing, but he seems to have lost his influence with the rabbis." This time there's no phone call. Teddy expresses support but is unable to help.

Item four: The Jewish Quarter. We want to flatten the roadway from Dung Gate to the Western Wall so people won't have such a steep climb coming into the square, but that means excavating and some religious groups have reacted with suspicion. "The trouble is," Teddy says, "every time we have your name associated with anything down there, suspicions erupt. We need to hide you in the closet. Why did we have your name on the drawings? We should have submitted them from the municipality. Let me see. Get Ephraim Shilo" (the coordinator for the Cabinet Committee for Jerusalem Affairs). "Ephraim, what are we going to do about this?"

While all this is going on, four or five people come in about other matters. Twenty minutes after we've begun, his press attaché comes in with the morning paper, gesturing at a headline about demonstrations by religious fanatics. Teddy gives instructions, returns to the discussion. Five minutes later comes a phone call. Ten minutes later the Deputy Mayor walks in. All matters are discussed openly. Sometimes my advice on planning matters is solicited, as I happen to be there.

After forty-five minutes we're up to Item 10. I leave with some assignments: letters to be written, matters to be followed up. Within forty-eight hours I will get back to Teddy with a report on the progress we have made.

This close relationship has been going on for fifteen years or more, beginning shortly after our first meeting in 1967. I cannot conceive of my commitment to work in Jerusalem as being independent from my particular relationship with its mayor.

Teddy Kollek talks slowly, thinking as he goes. He hates to give long speeches. At inaugurations and other occasions, I always know that when Teddy's turn comes he will say three sentences. He speaks a surprisingly simple Hebrew that is nevertheless extremely expressive. While he's generally quiet and soft-spoken, he has a sizable temper which has not mellowed over the last decade. Sometimes even the slightest irritation will cause an outburst of shouts and anger, not only in his office but during public appearances. On one occasion when he was heckled, he turned and told the hecklers to kiss his arse.

He has two shifts of secretaries. The morning shift starts with him at 5 a.m. Another shift comes in at midday and works until the afternoon. Then he usually goes to his office in the Israel Museum, where he has yet a third secretary who handles all his international correspondence. To make up for lost sleep, Teddy is notorious for stealing cat naps during the day. He has two kinds of naps — his public naps on grandstands and public stages when the speeches get boring and the naps that take place in policy meetings in his office when a dozen people might be gathered to discuss a critical issue. What is amazing is that he always wakes up at just that moment when the facts have been stated and a decision is about to be made. He opens his eyes and makes his decision. Is it possible that he heard the whole conversation?

CHAPTER 13

THE ONSLAUGHT OF THE RABBIS

In 1974 the Mamilla project and the Western Wall design were progressing well, but my relationship with the rabbis of the rabbinical college, Yeshivat Porat Yosef, was entering a new and potentially disastrous phase.

The architectural drawings were complete and the rabbis were out raising funds. They asked my office to provide drawings and photographs for a promotional brochure and to assign someone to design it. I wrote a short text that the rabbis supplemented. The text included a description of each room and every function of the building. In Israel, as elsewhere, the way to raise funds is first to sell the name of the building, then to sell each room to a donor and name it after him, and then, if you need still more money, to sell the seats, the entrances, the doors, and the doorknobs.

At first reading, I thought the rabbis' text was full of typing errors. For example, the dining room, which was to seat 300, was described as seating 400; the residences, which were to sleep 250, were described as having 350 beds. I made corrections and sent the proofs back.

A few hours later, I had an angry call from Rabbi Avraham Shrem. "Who do you think you are, changing the booklet?"

"I didn't change the booklet," I replied, "I just corrected the errors."

"What do you mean, errors? We will write what we want in the book."

"Well, we don't have three hundred fifty beds, we have two hundred fifty."

He said, "We will put four students in each room."

"They were designed for three, they won't accommodate four. And what about the dining room?" I responded.

"We'll crowd the dining room," he shouted back.

It became clear that they were exaggerating so as to have more and bigger rooms to sell to donors. The conversation ended abruptly: "We will print in our booklet what we want to print in our booklet."

That day was the turning point in my relations with the rabbis. Another day I went down to visit the construction site and found a new sign on the auditorium. The first three floors had been built, and as each new room was enclosed in concrete and stone, a sign would immediately go up, a plaque proclaiming that the auditorium — or the classroom or synagogue, as the case might be — was the gift of such and such a person in memory of someone. That day I noticed that some of the signs I had seen earlier in the week had disappeared and new signs with new names were being put up to replace them. I pointed to a sign and looked at the construction manager. He laughed and said, "Oh yes, new visitors are coming to see the rooms they have made contributions for. The rabbis move these signs around as new guests arrive."

During the same period, there came a cooling in relations between Stephen Shalom and the two rabbis. It rose first over the question of curriculum. Stephen Shalom was concerned that graduates of the yeshiva would be ill equipped to deal with communities in the United States and South America because of the limits of their education. He suggested that the rabbinical students should have a few hours a week of secular education — language, mathematics, that sort of thing. The rabbis rejected the proposal outright.

Stephen even went to the Ministry of Education and some other outside authorities in an attempt to press his conviction. This conflict started clouding the whole relationship. The authority vested in Stephen earlier was being withdrawn. Still, construction was advancing well, and the walls of the yeshiva had risen four or five storeys, when yet another conflict erupted. It concerned the concrete arches in the building.

The whole structure was conceived as a three-dimensional lattice of precast concrete arches connected by sophisticated joinery set within stone walls. For six months I had gone from quarry to quarry to find a stone the color of the Western Wall, which through aging had become a deep golden yellow. Most of the quarries yielded a lighter stone, which would have made the yeshiva stand out like a white Taj Mahal in the midst of its golden surroundings — clearly not what I was after. Near Hebron we finally found a suitable quarry.

The concrete in the arches would be made with the same stone. It took us another three months to mix the cement, an aggregate of finely crushed stone and sand. To achieve the appropriate finish for the concrete arches, we had to have just the right mix.

Somehow, the rabbis got it into their heads that precast arches were not as strong as monolithic ones. Someone had convinced them that the concrete should be "poured in place." In fact, the end product would be similar in strength whether precast or monolithic. But I resisted the change on principle. I feel that there should be a direct link between the method of construction and the form of a building. If the building is constructed of smaller pieces, the architecture should express that. If it is made of monolithic, poured-in-place concrete, the building should take on quite another form of continuous masses and surfaces. Adobe buildings, like those of poured-in-place concrete, are volumetric; their surface is continuous. One almost feels the motion of the trowels in the hands of those shaping the sufaces as they flow around soft corners from wall to ceiling. In contrast, Japanese wood construction is a fragmented assemblage of small pieces, exaggerating the joints and connections between beams, columns, and joists.

You can make Formica look like wood but everything about my education as an architect made me resist that kind of approach, just as it made me resist the change to poured-in-place arches. But after weeks of discussion, for the sake of shlom bayit (peace in the house) and for the sake of getting things moving again, I gave in.

As the arches were being poured in the residential wing, there was talk of reprogramming the stages of construction and it was suggested that the next phase be the synagogue. I was pleased because I was convinced that once the arched structure within the stone walls of the synagogue was completed, everyone, including the rabbis, would appreciate the quality of that room, and that in itself would defuse some of the disagreements.

At that point the rabbis called a meeting with one of their advisers, of which they had many. They asked him to interpret the plans of the synagogue. By now, they distrusted me so much that they felt it best to discuss the design with someone else. He explained the plans (without models) and concluded that the room would be poorly lit. He completely misunderstood the effect of top lighting by skylights.

The following day I went to a meeting with the rabbis. To my astonishment they began to question the entire concept of the synagogue they had previously approved. The model was set on the table. Avraham Shrem took the floor. "We never understood this plan before. Now it has been explained to us, we cannot accept it. It is all cluttered. Look at the model! What is this pyramid of arches, arches, and arches. There is no light."

I interrupted him: "Avraham, you have not been looking at this model properly. Please come, bend down, and look upwards." I pointed out the skylight. He interrupted me once more.

"No, no, no. This is not acceptable. This is an epidemic of arches."

I tried to keep calm. I pulled out the sectional drawing, once again pointing out the skylights, the mezzanines. They had, I reminded them, seen these models and drawings many times over a period of three years. They had in fact expressed great enthusiasm for the design when I had first presented it.

"No, it will never do!" he interrupted once more. "This is an opera house, not a synagogue." As the noise level in the room rose and my voice was added to the commotion, the other brother, Moshe, contributed his opinion that the design was more appropriate for a brothel.

To say I was dismayed would be a gross understatement. After years of expressing their delight with the synagogue's design, suddenly, this about-face. As usual, I never knew if this new objection expressed their true opinion or whether it was a tactic in the conflict with Stephen Shalom, the major benefactor whose father's name the synagogue would carry.

As if to throw further weight behind their position, they stated that they were not the only ones who didn't like the design — indeed, none other than the Chief Sephardic Rabbi of Israel, Rabbi Ovadia Yosef (a graduate of this yeshiva and its honorary president) had also objected to it.

I knew the Chief Rabbi and I was extremely doubtful that he had studied the design or expressed any opinion.

Nevertheless, wanting to resolve the situation, I said, "Well, if that's the way you feel, would you agree to my presenting him the designs with the model, and if he approves of it, then we can consider the matter settled?"

They would not commit themselves, but I asked the Chief Rabbi for a meeting and took the model along. Rabbi Yosef was about to undergo an operation for cataracts and could barely see. While he was extremely friendly during my visit, it was quite obvious that he did not want a confrontation with the Shrems. He blessed me, but on the subject of the yeshiva I left empty handed.

The next confrontation was over the stone arcades dividing the residences from the teaching complex. I had designed the main passageway of the building, framed in arches, to begin outside, continue through inside the building, then emerge once again on the exterior. The rabbis came to a meeting one day and said, "Look, you've got stone arcades on the outside. This we understand; people see it. But inside the building? Whoever heard of anyone using stone inside the building where the public can't see it?

I said, "You and the students will see it, and it will identify for you the fact that it is a principal passage. And besides, a corridor that is part stone, then plaster, then stone again would be ridiculous." I added that the stone arches were already three-quarters built, so there would be no savings in changing the design. But they were not convinced.

Three days later I received a phone call early in the morning from David Mitchell, my architect supervising construction at the yeshiva.

He was near panic. He stammered something about the building or the arches being demolished.

I ran over from my office in the Old City; David was waiting at the gates. He had come to the site in the morning, he told me, to find the entire arcade demolished. He led me inside. Stones were lying all over the ground. We asked the contractor's superintendent, who shrugged his shoulders in ignorance and embarrassment. Then we questioned the night watchman and wrung from him the unbelievable truth: in the middle of the previous night the rabbis had come and, using wood studs and tools they had found on the site, they had toppled and demolished the arches with their own hands.

David and I stood by the fallen stones. Some had broken from the impact of the fall. We looked at each other in silence. We had learned to expect almost anything from the rabbis, but we couldn't have imagined this.

Next, the rabbis said that the windows designed to fit into the arches need not be arched — they could be square! They asked the general contractor to install square windows, and of course he refused, saying he could build only in accordance with the architectural drawings. So they went to another contractor and ordered square windows. At 5 o'clock one morning, this contractor showed up on the site, without a word to the general contractor, and installed square windows in the openings where the arches had been!

That was the last straw. Next morning I called my lawyers, reviewed the contract with them, and asked them to get an immediate injunction from the district court to stop the rabbis from building anything that was not in accordance with the plans. A few days later, after hearing from both sides, the judge of the Jerusalem district court issued a temporary injunction and set the date for a hearing.

My travel schedule had me leaving the country in three days, meaning I'd miss the hearing. I decided to have my office manager, Dan Lansky, represent me, along with our lawyers. Back in Montreal four days later, I got a call from Lansky in the early morning Montreal time, minutes after he had left the court house. His voice was ecstatic, "We won!"

"It was Judge Landau," he said. "He kept smiling. Apparently he's from Haifa and knows much of your background. The rabbis were full of venom. Remember how they used to scream at you in meetings? They were at it again, saying that you were criminally negligent, that people can't live in your building, that people fall off the stairs . . . " As far as Judge Landau was concerned, the contract was absolutely clear and he made the injunction permanent.

It was also clear that the rabbis did not expect this outcome, in part because their lawyer, Shlomo Toussia-Cohen, rarely loses a case. They responded by not paying our fees.

When the contract was signed, the building was estimated at approximately twenty-one million Israeli pounds (at the time, about seven million dollars). In the second year of construction I asked the project manager to produce an up-to-date estimate of the value of the building so that I could submit a progress invoice. We hadn't been paid for many months, and most of the payments we had received came directly from Stephen Shalom, who had advanced some of his donations to the yeshiva directly to us.

It was now 1977, and inflation had brought the cost of the building to over forty million Israeli pounds (by then equal to eight million dollars), which meant additional fees were due. Even these additional fees did not cover our full costs: the building was unusually complicated; my travel expenses between Jerusalem and Montreal were not covered; and the construction had been delayed by the Yom Kippur War. Even if we had been paid what the contract called for at the time, my firm would still have had a deficit of two hundred and twenty-four thousand dollars on the job. We were not in fact paid until 1988, eleven years later.

Soon after we obtained the injunction, I initiated arbitration proceedings, as called for in the contract, asking the Institute of Architects and Engineers to appoint an arbitrator so that our fees might be paid. The man chosen was the retired chief planner of the city of Haifa, Joseph Cohen.

The rabbis told the arbitrator that I had designed an impossible building, a building that was unacceptable to them, and demanded payment of damages. They also asked him to rule on the design disagreements. The contract said that they had the right to ask for functional changes, and I was obliged to make them unless they went against my reasonable professional judgement. But the contract did not define "reasonable."

Simultaneously, the rabbis retaliated on the legal front.

They urged their lawyer to make an appeal to the Supreme Court of Israel and to drag out the arbitration as long as possible. The

Supreme Court deliberated at length. The three judges took the unprecedented action of leaving the court in order to visit the site. They ruled, first, that the contract was explicit and there was no way the client could make changes, thereby upholding the injunction; second, that even without that clause forbidding unapproved changes, they would have upheld the injunction because of the phrase the yeshiva lawyer had put in some years back: that they (the rabbis) were a body of laymen who knew nothing about building and vested in me full responsibility for design; and third, the judges called on the arbitrator to proceed with the arbitration.

Perhaps on the advice of their lawyer, or perhaps against it, the rabbis tried one more manoeuver. They wrote a letter firing me and then returned to the Supreme Court saying that, as the agreement with me was terminated, the clauses limiting our right to change the plans was null and void. The Court should therefore lift the injunction.

The Supreme Court ruled that the yeshiva could not fire me, for two reasons. First, the contract stated that if the work was terminated and then resumed, I had the right of first refusal to continue as architect (a clause I had completely forgotten). They went on to say that the rabbis' letter firing me was an attempt to circumvent a valid contract, and the court would not accept it.

At this point, the rabbis must have realized that they were going to have to turn to the arbitration process. Until then they had been calling in sick every time a meeting was scheduled and then rescheduling it for a time when they knew I would be out of the country.

These arbitration meetings, the rabbis with their attorney and I with mine, became a circus. They would start quietly enough with the presentation of some issue; then the rabbis' lawyer, Toussia-Cohen, would present their views in his civilized legal style. I would respond, and then it would be as if somebody had switched on a stereo at full volume, with everyone talking at once.

The rabbis became increasingly unpredictable. Rabbi Avraham Shrem would swear that he could not operate with one seat less than 450 in the study hall. One week later his brother, Rabbi Moshe Shrem, would concede they could make do with 350. Thus programmatic requirements stated as absolutely uncompromisable under any circumstances would become, a few months later, surprisingly flexible.

Finally, the big problem was the study hall (beit midrash). They claimed it cluttered up the entire plan and its location cut off light from the residential sections and some of the classrooms behind. Having spent all this money on what they said were the most beautiful arches in Jerusalem, they did not want to put up a study hall that would hide them. They had a new idea: to take the four storey synagogue and divide it into two rooms horizontally. The top room would be used for the study hall and the lower for the synagogue. The area originally intended for the study hall would be left as an open courtyard.

That would have been a radical change even before construction began. Now, with the buildings half built, it was virtually impossible. The floor size of the study hall would be limited to that of the synagogue below. Therefore it would never properly accommodate the 450 students. (The synagogue was designed to seat 300.)

There would also be access problems. The study hall had been placed next to the elevators and the central staircase, but in its new location, the students would have to go outdoors to get to it from the staircase. There were a lot of good reasons for thinking that particular change was unworkable.

Nonetheless, the arbitrator asked me to draw it up. I protested bitterly. It was a ridiculous solution functionally, and the issue was one of function. The arbitrator agreed with me but said he was a public servant who was responsible for seeing that the building got finished. If he ruled that the study hall stayed in its original location, building would stop and the yeshiva would remain a ruin. He ordered me to draw it up.

By then I was out of pocket several hundred thousand dollars, so I insisted that at least my expenses for the new drawings be covered. In three weeks I drew up the alternatives, prepared the models and drawings, and packed them all into an old-fashioned metal trunk, which I took with me to the next arbitration meeting.

Two days before the arbitration meeting I called my lawyer and said, "By now I know those rabbis. No matter what I show them, they will reject it and then they'll refuse to pay the fifteen thousand dollars. I want a cheque given to the arbitrator in trust before the meeting." I was being unreasonable, my lawyer told me. Nevertheless, I kept the trunk closed at the meeting and told the arbitrator that I wouldn't open it until he had the cheque in his hand.

For forty-five minutes I sat there calmly with the trunk locked while everybody screamed their heads off. At last the arbitrator took me aside and said he personally would take it upon himself to see that I was paid. "Open the trunk."

We all have our weak moments and that was mine. I opened the trunk and took out the drawings and model. (I got paid three years later, after countless requests.)

If a study hall accommodating 450 students was over the 300 seat synagogue, then the entire entrance of the yeshiva and the surrounding stone walls would have to be demolished.

Somewhat against my better judgement, I submitted the plans to the municipality for the building permits for the new stacked scheme, which called for the great demolition of the synagogue walls. At the same time I wrote a letter to the rabbis and to the arbitrator saying I was doing it under protest, using the Hebrew phrase that it would be "the cause of tears for generations."

This letter shook the arbitrator. He called a meeting and, to our surprise, for the first time made a number of decisions. He had decided that, even though he'd ruled in favor of the great demolition earlier, it was impractical and he now ruled against it.

However, he supported the rabbis' decision that the beit midrash should be built over the synagogue. But if this was done the beit midrash would have to be confined to the original envelope of the synagogue and therefore could accommodate only 300 students. If they needed space for more, they could use the synagogue chamber, giving them space for 600 students in two rooms.

Finally he ordered them to pay my outstanding fees immediately and asked me to produce a new set of construction plans.

Alternatives were priced and my original scheme (the magnificent synagogue in the glory of its four storeys and the study hall with its 400 seats) proved to be a million dollars cheaper than the stacked arrangement, with a synagogue that had no light and a smaller study hall without windows. Yet still the rabbis insisted that the second scheme was what they wanted.

Meanwhile, work had been continuing on the residential complex in accordance with the plans. One day I heard that they had moved 200 students into the building even though it was still far from complete. I suppose they may have thought that if the building was occupied and operations established, it would be harder for me to fight them.

For two weeks the students were in the building without plumbing. Then the contractor connected the plumbing, hooking the bathrooms and toilets into the city sewer system.

My instinct was to stay away but I knew I had to go and see what was going on. With David Mitchell, who was still supervising construction, I went to the site.

Suitcases were piled everywhere. Clothes hung across the windows to dry. Someone had threaded electrical wires on hooks in the walls all over the building; fluorescent tubes were hung haphazardly everywhere because the permanent lighting system had not been connected. Big pieces of plywood were nailed up to cover openings where railings had not yet been installed.

That is how the yeshiva is occupied to this day.

CHAPTER 14

PLANNING IN A DEMOCRACY

The months of planning Mamilla had evolved into years. It was now 1976 and we finally had a design, informally approved by city officials. We were ready to present it to the Jerusalem City Council. The Council meets in an oddly decorated chamber in City Hall. Strange fluorescent back-lit stained glass panels mimic windows. The councillors sit in a built-in circle in the centre of the room and chairs of every kind are scattered around the room for the press and other observers. Sloppily dressed waiters bring trays of Turkish coffee, soft drinks and sandwiches. The Mayor is forever banging his gavel and raising his voice to bring the councillors to order.

The Mayor had asked Meron Benvenisti, the newly appointed Deputy Mayor whose main official function was city planning, to present my Mamilla designs to the Council. His connections with Teddy Kollek went back many years: after the Six Day War, Benvenisti was put in charge of relations with the Arab community and helped to develop the Kollek administration's liberal, accommodating policies. He had written a book analyzing socio-political developments in Jerusalem during the years immediately after unification.

Mayor Teddy Kollek opened the meeting, briefly tracing the history of the project from its beginnings in 1972 down to the recent approval, in principle, by the sub-committee on planning. Now, the detailed plans were being presented for the full Council's approval.

The Mayor continued, his voice firm (if somewhat monotonous), "A lot of progress has been made in clearing the site. More than half the families living in slum conditions have been resettled in new neighborhoods. Many businesses, particularly the workshops, have been relocated to other industrial zones." The Mayor finished by noting: "There are private investors who are interested in proceeding with the project."

For the next half hour Benvenisti was silent as several councillors spoke, some for and some against the project. Those in favor spoke of the contribution the project would make to the image of Jerusalem. "Conditions at Jaffa Gate," said one, "are unbearable — the trucks, the parking, the buses. Something must be done to serve the Old City immediately."

"Yes — it's a blemish on the image of Jerusalem! We can't have a slum dominating the pilgrims' entry to the city," another chimed in.

Opposing councillors questioned the project's financial soundness: "Can we really afford it?" and "Isn't there a danger that construction might begin without the funds to complete it, as happened with the central bus station in Tel Aviv?"

Benvenisti's silence heightened tension in the room.

I noticed the Mayor's discomfort. He had spent many hours reviewing the project with Benvenisti and me, doing all he could to convince him of its value. He now expected Benvenisti's support, and the prolonged silence was alarming him.

I was also on tenterhooks. We had developed the Mamilla plan in close collaboration with the municipality; every line drawn had their support; everything had been done in a spirit of consensus. But right after the project had been approved by the previous Council, the Mayor had forced the retirement of the city engineer, the man responsible for planning up to that time. Benvenisti was, in effect, a new client for the project.

Benvenisti was in his early forties then, a big man, very energetic and emotional, with a thick head of curly black hair, slightly graying, and a forceful voice and manner. Liberal, highly educated, indeed a scholar, he is not the kind of person one usually encounters in municipal government. In the early 1970s, he proposed organizing Jerusalem into a series of boroughs with a high degree of self-government. This gave the Arab residents more of a say in their own affairs, a policy that Kollek has supported ever since, but it brought strong reactions from Jewish nationalists, who went around painting "Benvenisti the Traitor" on Jerusalem's walls.

I would have expected him to be sympathetic to our design, which was innovative but also conservationist and minimalist. It was far from massive, and it was sympathetic to Mamilla's potential impact on Jewish-Arab relations in the city. Benvenisti was also loyal to the Mayor, who strongly supported the project.

An hour after the beginning of the meeting, an opposing councillor became particularly vociferous over the plans, questioning whether they were an appropriate priority for city funds. "We have other more important tasks to tackle before Mamilla," he thundered, and began questioning its economic feasibility.

I sprang to my feet and was recognized by the Mayor. Somewhat emotionally, I voiced my sense of urgency about the project and reiterated that the private sector would be funding most of it. I reminded them of Mamilla's pivotal role in creating a truly united city. My intervention seemed to antagonize Benvenisti, who sprang to his feet, breaking his silence at last.

"I have had a heavy heart about this project for some time. I recognize that many years of effort have gone into its conception and implementation. I recognize also that my predecessors have reviewed and approved it."

He paused.

"But my conscience would not be clear," he went on, "and I would not be fulfilling my responsibilities, if I did not express my opposition!"

He began by questioning the priorities. He claimed that the final burden would be on the public purse. Even if funds were promised by the central government, this was money that would otherwise be spent for other projects in Jerusalem.

This argument was unduly pessimistic. Benvenisti seemed to lack confidence in anything dependent on private enterprise.

He added that he found the project overly ambitious, even apart from the question of financial priorities. If Mamilla Street was built underground, he argued, it would be difficult to build it in stages as market demand developed and resources became available. The city would be forced to do it all at once.

The Mayor sat there silent and depressed. From his point of view the dispute transcended Mamilla. It was not simply a disagreement with his Deputy Mayor over a project, it was the breaking of ranks.

I looked over toward Eliezer Ronnen, who sat a few seats away from me, his big cigar jutting out as usual from under his great moustache, his brown suit an anomaly among the many shirtsleeves. When Meron started talking, our eyes met, and he rolled his in an expression of disbelief. The two men had been members of the City Council. Both were men of the left. Both, however, were keenly competitive about the roles they were to play in the development of Jerusalem, and each had political aspirations at the national level. They had each been interested in heading Karta (the corporation set up to develop central Jerusalem and Mamilla) when it was formed, but the Mayor chose Ronnen as chairman of Karta and Benvenisti as Deputy Mayor in charge of planning.

Despite Benvenisti's opposition at that critical meeting, the Council did approve the plan with a few modifications and sent it to the District Planning Commission. Thus I went about refining the plans and translating them into an official document for approval.

After this, I found myself spending a lot of time trying to defuse tensions between Benvenisti and Ronnen. They did the most ridiculous things to annoy one another. I found my role expanding from architect to diplomat; I felt like the Kissinger of Mamilla. From time to time, when the tension got unbearable, the Mayor would summon everybody to a meeting and there would be peace and understanding, sometimes for as long as forty-eight hours

While Benvenisti continued to rally the opponents to the project, Ronnen succeeded in navigating it through one obstacle after another, ensuring the constant flow of funds, primarily for the resettlement of residents. He also got the approval of an endless series of committees, ministries, and other government authorities.

Projects are always shaped by the principal actors involved, particularly those projects that evolve over the years. Now, as if Mamilla had not had sufficient drama with Benvenisti's appearance, yet another actor was to make a grand entrance. Except this time, I seem to have been the catalyst for his introduction.

For months, the Jerusalem Committee had been urging the Mayor to hire a new city engineer to direct the city's planning, replacing the one who had retired. It occurred to me that one of my closest friends, a Tel Aviv architect and planner, Amnon Niv, might be the right person for the job and I recommended him to the Mayor and Benvenisti. He had a thriving practice in Tel Aviv, but welcomed this chance to diversify his activities and thought he could divide his time between the two cities.

Teddy Kollek met with Amnon and they hit it off. Benvenisti, after two or three long meetings with him, soon endorsed his appointment. His arrival in Jerusalem opened a third chapter in the life of Mamilla.

Meanwhile, Benvenisti continued to oppose the project, raising one new issue after the other: it was within the National Park boundaries; it was costly; it was inflexible; the list continued to grow. Suddenly and unexpectedly, the polemics were followed by action. Benvenisti recruited a young architect in the city planners department, David Kroyanker, and either permitted or instructed him to develop an alternative plan for Mamilla.

I heard rumblings about Kroyanker's plan but found it too fantastic to believe that the Deputy Mayor would try to undermine a plan approved by the Council by initiating a new one. But just a few days before our refined plan was scheduled for review by the District Committee on October 9, 1976, Benvenisti and Kroyanker announced their plan and distributed a lavishly printed copy of it to the press.

One feature of the Kroyanker plan was that it preserved almost all the buildings in Mamilla in a kind of quaint "gaslight" town. This meant the Valley of Hinnom could not be cleared of buildings, excavated, and made into a park. What is more, Kroyanker cut off the new centre from Jaffa Gate with an open four-lane highway, clearly separating the Old City from the new.

To the Mayor, Benvenisti's action was politically and personally intolerable. The schism between them could not be repaired. Weeks went by without a word passing between them. And then, suddenly, Benvenisti resigned.

Not long afterwards, Benvenisti left Israel to work on his Ph.D. at Harvard, where he wrote a dissertation on bicultural cities in conflict. Michal and I were living in Boston when a mutual friend mentioned that he was at the Kennedy School. I telephoned to invite him over. He told me: "I still feel very bitter about Mamilla. You won the battle, but I have not got over the consequences. There's no way I'll come and have coffee with you."

It was not until several years later, in 1981, that the Middle Eastern traditional sulcha (Arabic for "peacemaking") took place between us. We were both asked to appear in a face-to-face television debate about Mamilla one Friday evening, telecast live from Herzliya. The network, perhaps by design, arranged for one of those large Mercedes taxis to pick us both up in Jerusalem.

When the taxi arrived at my door Benvenisti and his wife were already in it and we spent the next seventy-five minutes together driving to the studio in Herzliya. At first conversation was very stiff but slowly it loosened up somewhat. On TV we had a good debate. Benvenisti said that he always thought Mamilla to be a wonderful plan; his problem was never the architecture but the priorities of public spending. Our conversation became more friendly during the drive back to Jerusalem, and since then he has helped my students at Harvard on several projects related to Jerusalem.

Benvenisti's departure ought to have opened the way for execution of the Mamilla plans. But this was not to be.

By now, Amnon Niv was firmly entrenched in his position. With no immediate replacement for Meron, he was his own boss. He decided to summarize his feelings about Mamilla in a working paper, a copy of which he sent me.

It was a devastating critical assessment of my design. Niv thought the underground road system was too costly, and he reiterated Benvenisti's point that it made the project rigid since it would all have to be done at once. But he went further than Benvenisti, suggesting the project be designed so that it could be broken up into small parcels, each of which could be turned over to a small developer, rather than depending on one or two large developers to implement the whole scheme.

The most painful aspect of this turn of events was the personal one. It just hit me in too vulnerable a spot. This was not just some city official questioning a project; this was one of my closest friends.

He explained that as a private architect he could enjoy the project's design qualities, but as a city engineer he saw only the obstacles. On several occasions, he protested that, although painful for him to take, his actions were for the good of the project.

The time had come for me to make some hard decisions. I knew that at this juncture, without Niv's support, there was no hope of realizing the project as I had designed it.

As I agonized over what to do, I began to see that the underground road did make the project more complicated to implement and the phases more rigid. If there was a way of solving the traffic problem without the underground roads, I knew much of the opposition would be defused.

I also had to consider a new issue that had emerged in the recent public discussions — the preservation of the old buildings. In the early 1970s, the idea that the monastery church and surrounding buildings should be preserved and the rest demolished was generally accepted. But now, in 1977, attitudes were different. The Council for a Beautiful Israel and the Society for the Protection of Nature in Israel had been vigorously campaigning to save most of the buildings in Mamilla. Niv's suggestion that the project be broken into small components was in response to this campaign.

Keeping in mind this change in the public attitude, I convinced Ronnen to let me have a crack at a major revision of the plan. I then initiated a series of working meetings with Niv. If we wanted to get the project going, something had to give. Besides, as is often the case, I had changed some of my ideas over time. The project had begun nearly six years earlier, and I had developed and evolved personally over those years. I was also exhausted. If we could get going with a less perfect plan, so be it.

I decided to eliminate the underground road which was to have been built under Mamilla Street, and move it into the valley within the proposed park. This meant that Mamilla Street as it existed would be closed to traffic and become a pedestrian mall, and the two levels of shops could be built either at once or in phases. Once this was done, the only covered road would be at Jaffa Gate where it would descend under a pedestrian piazza to connect Mamilla with the Old City.

I also went back for a more careful look at the buildings. On the northern side of Mamilla Street were a few buildings of considerable charm and richness of detail, so I decided to make an effort to preserve the streetfront portion of these buildings, giving the new Mamilla a patina of the older days.

After an intensive eight week effort in Boston I came back with a brand-new set of drawings and a new model. The model differed in technique from the earlier ones. Before, we had elaborately detailed the windows, arcades, railings, etc., but people became distracted by insignificant details — whether they liked that many arched or square windows, for example. We made the new model without any architectural details so that it showed only the massing. It was a low-key, unexciting model, and it stirred up much less opposition.

The new plan was finished just in time for a meeting of the Jerusalem Committee, and after the presentation, they encouraged us to proceed. That lightened my heart, because I felt I had made a great compromise for the sake of realizing the project.

In fact I was delighted. But not for long. Those who had said we weren't preserving enough buildings did not drop their opposition; nor did those who were against underground roads even though that feature had been eliminated. Mamilla had become a cause célèbre.

The focus of the new attack was Jaffa Road. In the revised plan we proposed that the existing Jaffa Road running parallel to the city wall should be widened from three to four lanes. The opposition said the heavy traffic on this road would cause vibrations that would endanger the stability of the wall. But, we explained, the new road would not be as steep and therefore would cause less vibration and less pollution, as confirmed by experts from the Technion.

The opponents now recruited another city employee to their cause. Arthur Kutcher, an architect who had earlier published a critical book on planning in Jerusalem, made a drawing of Jaffa Road as it dipped under the pedestrian platform at Jaffa Gate — looking like the Long Island Expressway heading straight for the Old City. Since this didn't look bad enough, he added a great big freeway sign with an arrow, reading "Shopping Centre." He then took a photographer to the site of the heavily travelled road beside the wall, but instead of standing where he made his drawing (at the centre of the existing road) he moved twenty feet closer to the wall, where there is now a landscaped path. The photograph, with bushes hiding the road and traffic, implied that no road existed there.

The opponents then took their story to the Jerusalem correspondent of the *New York Times*, David Shipler. On Monday morning the article with the photo and drawing appeared on the front page: "Israel's Plan to Build Near Wall in Spite of Warnings." There was no mention that the drawing had been made by an opponent of the project. Everyone who saw it assumed that they were looking at a proposal for a new road on virgin land running into a tunnel under the Old City. All sorts of people fired off telegrams.

The Mayor was furious. But the *New York Times* article had striking and unexpected results. In Israel, people are divided until outsiders interfere. The story stirred up the members of the District Planning Committee. The road was changed from four lanes to two, it was moved one metre westward, and the revised plan was approved within two weeks. The Mayor and Niv fired Kutcher.

It has been suggested that this constant modification of the Mamilla plans is the inevitable consequence of planning in a democracy. People argue that the initial Mamilla plan in 1973 was too much the result of a single vision, which also required a single central authority to implement it, not to mention considerable economic resources. In comparison, the revised plan of 1978 is pluralistic in that it can accommodate a variety of developments and is sufficiently fragmented that it can be implemented by several agencies over a long period of time, depending on resources.

Is a plan better when it gives way to the diversity of views of a pluralistic process, editing out any strong "big" idea in favor of the more fragmented implementation and appearance of the multiplicity of interpretations? Can one say that the pluralistic plan is more humane, more friendly?

The problem in accepting the pluralistic solution is that it ignores the fact that some of the greatest and most admired urban places could not have been achieved through this contemporary version of due process. Surely there would be no great crescent in Bath, Grosvenor Square in London, Galleria Vittorio Emanuele II in Milan, Piazza Navona in Rome, Connaught Place in New Delhi, or even the great Maidan in Esfahan, and I would dare say even Central Park in New York. These would have been subjugated to the pluralistic process of planning. The idea of public consultation and community boards is fraught with its own sense of distortion. The process tends to be dominated by those fearful of change because people cling to the familiar, and those opposing an idea are, by nature, more vocal than those supporting one. Those prepared to take the risk of change are not always heard.

Years ago, I was fascinated to discover in the archives of Montreal emotional letters opposing the purchase of that distant parcel of land proposed as Mont Royal Park. Today the park is at the very heart of the city. I am certain there are similar documents concerning Central Park and every other major urban intervention. Obviously we need an appropriate balance between big ideas and piecemeal incremental development.

The Roman and Greek cities achieved this balance admirably. The city was given a sense of order and orientation through the monumental but integrated design of its main thoroughfares and piazzas. The Cardo Maximus and Décumanus, unified by repetitive singular colonnades and stoae, the great agoras — these are the result of a single building authority in the city. This was balanced by the rather unstructured conglomeration of atrial housing and workshops, as random in pattern as most Mediterranean villages of today.

The pluralistic mechanism of planning by consensus is incapable of giving us this kind of balance. Unfortunately, the level of distrust in public intervention has become so great, perhaps as a result of chronic abuse, that we must search for a new level of agreement and understanding before the current impotence can be corrected.

CHAPTER 15

IN SEARCH OF A DEVELOPER

The next thing that Mamilla needed was a developer with expertise in central city mixed-use developments. All my experience in working on projects of the scale of Mamilla in the United States and Canada convinced me that it was essential to include one in the planning process, and the larger the project, the more important the developer's input could be.

I was then, in 1978, in the process of moving my main office from Montreal, where it had been since Habitat '67, to Boston. Faneuil Hall Marketplace was one of the locations which I was considering — in fact the one I finally chose. It was one of the turning points in the planning and development of American cities, the first successful major downtown shopping centre. Located in several historic buildings, it was to me a demonstration of the sensitivity of the architect, Ben Thompson, and the developer, the Rouse Company. I put the Rouse Company forward as the ideal type of developer for Mamilla.

Local developers in Israel had built several large-scale mixed-use projects over the past twenty years, and all had been social and commercial failures. Some of the opposition to Mamilla arose out of the bad impressions these other developments had made. They opened to the public with construction incomplete and with half the shops empty. Poorly maintained, they failed to draw the public from nearby conventional shopping streets. Little thought had been given to understanding the problems of access, marketing, pedestrian movement, traffic patterns, and merchandising.

In the United States and Canada developers retain ownership of a centre. They lease the space in accordance with a plan for a balanced mix of shops, and once the centre is operating they continue to fine tune it, removing and replacing retailers as experience proves necessary, and completely controlling advertising and maintenance.

I decided to visit Jim Rouse in Maryland, in the new town of Columbia, which his company had built. I had been there five years before, when he had worked with me on Coldspring New Town, and I was surprised how well Columbia had filled in. Jim Rouse's office, an attractive white three storey stucco building with wood trellises, adjacent to other office buildings, was set beside a man-made lake. The trees had grown taller, the lake seemed more natural.

I went up to Jim's office. We walked out onto the terrace and as we looked across the lake, he remarked how Columbia had become a real town. He reminded me how skeptical everyone had been in the beginning, assuming that it would just be another dormitory town, but now there were more jobs in Columbia than there were residents.

We sat down in his office and he asked me what I was doing. I told him about Jerusalem and showed him some Mamilla drawings. Then I asked him, "Do you know Jerusalem?"

He shook his head. So I asked, "Well, Jim, would you like to come over and see it — if you were the official guest of the Mayor?"

He looked at me in surprise, then said, "If the Mayor invites me, why not?"

Jim Rouse is an unusual mixture of businessman, visionary, and idealist. Sixty-four then, with thinning hair combed back, he bears a remarkable resemblance, particularly in his smile and manner of speaking, to the actor James Stewart. He speaks with passion and one is moved by his belief in his vision. The Rouse Company came into being partly due to his financial skills and partly due to his prophetic vision. He pioneered the idea of building new communities on virgin land beyond the suburbs and of bringing downtown back

164

to life. He conceived Columbia as a way of creating a better environment in a country that was being devastated by suburban sprawl, and he showed his courage by developing Faneuil Hall Marketplace even though many financial institutions refused to finance it.

A few hours after my visit to Jim Rouse I telephoned Teddy Kollek at midnight (seven in the morning Jerusalem time) and told him something about the Rouse Company. Would he invite Rouse to Israel as his guest? He said he would be delighted to, and he added, "Could you call Ronnen and see if Karta can pick up the tab?"

Karta did, and a few weeks later I met the Rouses at Ben Gurion airport. Jim, his wife Patty, and his family did not know much about the history of the country. As we took the forty mile drive from the airport to Jerusalem, they asked me to fill in some of the details. At Bab el Wad, the entrance to the mountain pass, we drove past rusting half-destroyed armored cars, remnants of the convoys of the War of Independence of 1948, all preserved as memorials to those who died breaking the siege of Jerusalem.

In 1972 I had done my accelerated conscription service in the Israeli army (having left at age fifteen for Canada, I finally fulfilled my obligation at age thirty-three). The army, conscription, the wars, are part of the personal experience of almost every Israeli.

I told them how the fighting had been particularly bitter in and around Jerusalem. During a long siege, the Jewish population was cut off from the coastal zone, and for a time it seemed that severe shortages of food and water might force the surrender of the whole city to the Arab Legion. The siege was eventually broken by the construction of a bypass road through the mountains (Israel's version of the Burma Road), following the path of an old Roman road.

We passed a soldiers' hitchhiking station, and I noticed the surprised look on the Rouses' faces as they saw dozens of uniformed young men and women, fully armed, waiting in line to hitchhike. I explained that yes, there was conscription for both sexes — three years for men, two years for women. I sorted out for them the different wars: 1948, the War of Independence when the State of Israel was formed; 1956, Sinai, lasting some nine days; 1967, the Six Day War when Jerusalem was reunified, and the West Bank, Golan Heights and Sinai came under Israeli control; 1973, the Yom Kippur War, when Israel was taken by surprise on its most sacred holiday and had to fight for eighteen days before recapturing the territories it had taken in the Six Day War.

Soon we arrived at the city and drove to the King David Hotel, from which the Jaffa Gate is visible across the Valley of Hinnom. On the way, I told them about the afternoon in 1946 when my cousins and I (age eight) ventured out into an already tense city. In reaction to the British order to halt all immigration, terrorist activities of the Jewish nationalist groups were stepping up. The British administrative centre at the end of Jaffa Street, surrounded by many layers of barbed wire, had been converted to "Bevingrad". (Ernest Bevin had been Britain's Foreign Secretary at the end of the British Mandate period.) Other British offices were set up in the south wing of the King David Hotel, and their soldiers were everywhere, on foot and in armoured cars.

Standing near Jaffa Gate, looking toward the west, my cousins and I suddenly saw an enormous cloud of fire and smoke belching out of the King David Hotel. In what seemed to be absolute silence, the building crumbled before our eyes. A second later, we heard the enormous bang of the explosion. At that moment the city went wild with screaming sirens, running soldiers, and careening fire trucks.

So here was a city where Jews and Arabs and British regularly shopped together on Ben Yehuda Street and frequented the same public places and movie houses. Yet it was also a city where two British deserters helped blow up Ben Yehuda Street with three explosive-filled trucks, where Jewish terrorists blew up a wing of the King David Hotel, and Arab terrorists massacred Jews on many occasions. Jerusalem was one city then, but these events were symbols of its fragility.

For the next eight days I spent almost sixteen hours a day with the Rouses, walking with them through the historic sites, rediscovering Jerusalem through their eyes. Jim always wants to find out everything. In the Holy Sepulchre, he wanted to explore every crevice, every room, even the roof. At the vegetable suq (market), he wanted to follow every alley and dead-end path.

Our visits to the less glamorous retail and commercial centre of the downtown impressed me most, because it was like being present at an in-depth market study. This analysis was conducted not through a series of questionnaires and statistical compilations, but in the mind of a single person. All the factors — the merchandise, the pricing, the rents, the demand, the competitions, the size of shops — were processed by Jim's internal computer. You could see him study and explore all the details step by step.

We went into shop after shop. He would ask whether they owned the store, what their rent was, and check the inventory and prices. We visited appliance shops, book shops, clothing stores, and I soon discovered that his insight into the problems of downtown Jerusalem was superior to that of most market analysts and economists.

He immediately pinpointed the highly uncompetitive nature of the retail situation. The downtown was locked in by residential neighborhoods, so there were fewer stores than would ordinarily be found in a city of this size. By talking to customers in the stores he found that they did a great deal of their shopping in Tel Aviv because there was not enough variety in Jerusalem. He commented on the shabby displays in the shop windows, and he was surprised by the high prices, the low quality, and the frequently very poor service.

Finally we met with the Karta board in its domed conference room. Rouse was expecting to face, as he often had in the United States, a formal group in pin-striped suits, sitting on Eames leather chairs around a table in a wood panelled room. The Karta board was made up of public officials, directors of public companies, a Deputy Minister, and a member of the board of Bank Leumi. However, in true Israeli fashion, they were informally dressed, no ties or jackets, and were chatting informally. Refreshments were scattered around the plain utilitarian table.

Jim began his presentation. He said Mamilla was one of the best sites he'd ever seen for the vital centre of a city — it was the "100% corner" of Jerusalem. Few projects he'd engaged in had those advantages of location, access, and attractiveness. He went on to say that when his firm was brought into a project that had already been designed, they were generally forced to redesign it from scratch. In this project, he added (to my delight), he did not want to change a single detail.

What Jerusalem needed in Mamilla was the contemporary re-creation of the suq experience. He did not propose, for example, thirty-five foot wide malls, as in Columbia, but arcades only slightly wider than the Old City Markets.

"But Mr. Rouse," one board member asked, "don't you think a project of this size would threaten those very suqs which you find so unique?"

"No, it's different merchandise."

"Then what about our downtown merchants?" another member interrupted.

He smiled, "They were worried about that in Baltimore, they were worried about that in Boston at Faneuil Hall. In fact, the very opposite was the case — new business was generated for everyone around. Mamilla would do the same for your downtown. In fact in the absence of competition, I found your retail markets stagnant.

"I'd say your residents are not getting a good deal. The high rents of downtown shops prove there is a serious shortage of retail space. Mamilla would not only improve shopping for Jerusalemites but would bring about the improvement of the entire downtown shopping district. It might even bring Tel Aviv shoppers to Jerusalem."

"For Mamilla to be a real success," he went on, "I think it must open a new chapter in retailing in Israel. That means not simply building shops and renting or selling them but actively creating new merchants, putting people into business. We've done that in our other projects."

It was all music to my ears, and to Ronnen's. James Rouse had confirmed, even beyond our expectations, the validity of our ideas and hopes for the site. For a moment, it seemed as if nothing could stop us.

But as Ronnen proceeded with high level discussions with potential developers around the world, intrigue set in. (Rouse felt it was unlikely his company would venture outside the U.S. and was acting only as an adviser.) Ronnen, like me, was placing a great deal of emphasis on finding a private developer for Mamilla. This soon brought him into an increasingly tangled conflict with influential members of Karta, who were critical of the way he was managing the negotiations.

One member, a director of Israel's largest bank, was convinced that Karta itself could act as the developer, financed by a public stock offering. He felt that developers would simply come in, reap the benefits, and contribute little. Ronnen countered that a developer was needed not only primarily for funding, but for know-how.

As often happens in Israel, difference of opinion soon turned into broader personal conflicts. This last eruption found Mayor Kollek more impatient than usual. He had seen Ronnen clash with the first city engineer in 1972. He had seen him clash with Benvenisti in 1974. After all the other battles, he was simply too exhausted for yet another round of arguments. Teddy's reaction was simply to stop communicating.

The worst blow came from Ronnen himself: he sent in his letter of resignation. He felt he could not function while the Mayor and his two advisers (who were on Karta's board) constantly criticized his every move without giving him the opportunity to respond.

Perhaps he hoped the Mayor would ask him to stay and that his resignation would lead to a confrontation that would mend their relations. Whatever the motivation, I could not understand his action. He had nursed the project for ten years, brought it to the verge of realization, and now this.

Teddy Kollek immediately accepted Ronnen's resignation and told me in private that he rejected any kind of ultimatum. The resignation seemed to me more an act of desperation than an ultimatum but Teddy was also bitter about the timing. It was now just a few weeks before an election that would decide the fate of the Begin government. Ronnen's resignation meant that his successor would be appointed by a new Minister of Housing, and this might reduce the city's influence on the project. The Mayor thought that if Mamilla had been important enough to Ronnen he would never have chosen this moment to resign.

Ronnen's departure left a real void. We had worked together for nine years. We had our share of arguments, but we became good friends. Most important, we shared the same fundamental values. We were both motivated by similar dreams and convictions. We both believed in the Mayor's policy and vision of Jerusalem as a city in which diverse people live together in cooperation and deal with each other in spite of their differences. Ronnen and I both believed that Mamilla, as a new centre for Jerusalem, was a manifestation of these policies. This was not just another urban renewal project or some vacant land that needed to be filed with new buildings. It was an opportunity to create a new centre to connect and bridge the old and new city, Arabs and Israelis. It would be a real meeting place, an urban living room, a public garden, all of which the city urgently needed, and it was strategically located.

I was not sure if I would be able to continue the battle alone. I had the Mayor on my side but he had many other issues to attend to. With Ronnen's departure, I felt almost solely responsible for Mamilla, a lonely feeling. I realized that seeing it through was going to take formidable patience, which no school of architecture could have prepared me for.

Urban design is not architecture. It deals with many more variables. An urban design plan takes much longer than realizing any building designed by an architect. Perhaps more than any other endeavour, urban design demands patience, a stubborn perseverance, and an ever-flowing spring of optimism. My students at Harvard often ask me about the differences. I tell them the most important thing is to start young enough to see a plan through.

CHAPTER 16

THE HEBREW UNION COLLEGE

Jerusalem is a city of courtyards, each courtyard having its own distinct character. Courtyards differ as the faces of human beings differ. The proportions, the elements that form the edges, the materials of construction and the plant life, all make the design of a courtyard the least understood and the least appreciated element of building. Some believe that merely deciding to put a courtyard in a building is in itself meaningful. But it is the making of a great courtyard that is the challenge.

Nowhere in the city are the courtyards as diverse and wholesome as they are in the Armenian Quarter. As I came to enjoy the Armenian Quarter, I also came to know some of the leading members of the community. One day, Archbishop Ajamian, a leader of the Armenian community, invited me to lunch. He was proposing developing some land on the Mount of Olives. I welcomed any excuse to visit his quarter.

From Jaffa Gate, I followed the narrow road which runs right against the city wall. As a tourist taxi roared by, I squeezed against an arch and suddenly found myself at the small opening in front of the large doors to the Armenian Quarter. How easy for the uninitiated to miss that simple door that is the principal entrance to a Quarter that houses some 2,000 souls. A monk on duty in a black cassock and several children at play chatting in Armenian, were the only hint that anything was behind it.

I passed through the gate into a small courtyard the forecourt of St. James Cathedral. First built in the fifth century, St. James is the oldest continuously used church in the world. A small archway on the right led to a larger courtyard where austere structures on either side were pierced by small openings with ornate grills attached. Ahead were three great archways leading to another courtyard, and at the right was an elegant, self-supporting stone spiral stair. Three cypress trees clustered at the corner. Rows of small rough stones, forming the ancient floor of the courtyard, shimmered like sunlight reflecting on the sea.

I walked through into a triangular court whose central garden was filled with trees and flowers. On each side were deep arcades, two storeys high, behind which doors led into the rooms — one of the seminaries of the Armenians.

A steep stair led me up to the roof, where a view of the city skyline unveiled itself — the Holy Sepulchre to the north, the structures on the Temple Mount to the east, the tower of the Citadel to the west. I crossed one roof, then made my way over a little bridge to another roof. There I found a terrace surrounded by vines, trees planted in pots, and a small doorway into the residence of Archbishop Ajamian.

The Archbishop's house was modest but filled with treasures, icons, illuminated manuscripts, and other ancient objects that he showed me with great pride. It was not clear whether the house and the treasures belonged to him or to the church. A lunch of delicious Armenian delicacies arrived: stuffed zucchinis, aubergines, and meats with spices different from the ones found in other quarters.

Over lunch I talked with the Archbishop about how the Armenian Quarter is completely different in architecture and urban structure from the rest of the Old City. Where the Muslim Quarter is a series of intricate alleys punctuated by roofs and small domestic courtyards, the Armenian Quarter is more like the cities of Italy or Spain. It has a series of majestic public spaces — courtyards distinctly made for the collective public life — behind which are hidden yet another layer of small domestic courtyards. These courtyards, each with its own personality — one entirely paved, another lush with climbing bougainvillea and jasmine, another surrounding the cathedral — create a sequence of what I would call "city rooms" around which the life of the community is centred.

Ajamian, with his elegant goatee, black gown, sash, and a little bit of a pot belly, smiled with pleasure. What fascinated me, I told him, was how particular and different these spaces were from other parts of the Old City. "We have been here since the fifth century," he said. "This place has been built step by step as a single community."

Some of the most successful courtyards in Jerusalem are products of the nineteenth and twentieth centuries. I remember going to a party given in honor of Mayor Kollek's seventieth birthday in the courtyard of the Rockefeller Museum, a building designed in 1927 by the British architect Austin St. Barbe Harrison.

In the museum's rectangular courtyard, long tables lit by candles and laden with wonderful foods and fruits were arranged for the four hundred guests from all over the world. A paved gallery set back above the massive arcade ran around the four sides. Water lilies floated in a still, long pool at the centre of the courtyard. A classical quartet played baroque music at one end of the courtyard, later to be relieved by two folk singers. On that moonless summer evening, the sky was filled with stars.

No room could have created the ambience of that night in the courtyard. No ceiling, however exquisite, could match that natural dome of sky and stars. I'd had many such experiences in Jerusalem's courtyards by the time I came to design some of my own.

My chance came in 1975. The Hebrew Union College, the educational arm of the American Jewish Reform Movement, was proposing a large expansion for their modest Jerusalem campus. I had met Richard Scheuer, the chairman of the board of governors and its building committee, in New York when the Jewish Museum, which he also headed, exhibited for everyone a garden, an exhibition on my work. Some time later, Scheuer and I, with Alfred Gottschalk, Hebrew Union College's president, walked around the proposed site on King David Street, outside the walls of the Old City. We spoke about the building and the Reform Movement. In the United States the movement had emerged in the second half of the nineteenth century, started mostly by Jews of German origin who had attempted to adapt Halachic Judaism to the realities and conditions of contem-

173

porary life. Eccentric interpretations of biblical edicts were modified — for example, those that forbid the use of cars or electricity on the Sabbath. In the Reform synagogue, men and women pray together (as they do in Conservative synagogues) and are not physically separated as in Orthodoxy. The Reform Movement has been strongly opposed by the Orthodoxy, who seem at times to be threatened by it as much as by Christian missions. They have fought any attempt to give the movement legitimacy or presence in Israel. This conflict introduced a tension into the project.

From the outset, the governing boards of the Hebrew Union College were worried that their efforts to build a major campus in Jerusalem might be thwarted by the Orthodox. After the preliminary sketches for the campus were produced, there was a delay in the execution of the ninety-nine year lease of the land from the state to the college.

Their lawyer in Jerusalem insisted that this was "normal bureaucracy" and that it would take many months to get all the different agencies and the land authority to resolve the many conditions attached to the agreement. One condition, for example, was that buildings would be constructed within five years of transferring the land. Alfred Gottschalk and Richard Scheuer, however, did not view the delay as innocent bureaucracy. They thought it was deliberate.

I too was concerned. When I began selecting engineering consultants for the job, I identified a particular firm to submit a proposal for structural design. They declined with embarrassment. "You know," they said, "many of our projects are for Orthodox institutions. This project might affect our livelihood. We cannot participate."

But for a while we continued to work. Scheuer explained that the campus expansion was ambitious and that it would be built in phases, as funds became available. The classrooms would come first, then the study centre, archaeological museum and facilities for registering and researching artifacts. The administrative headquarters for the World Union for Progressive Judaism might be included, as well as a reception centre for visiting pilgrims (mostly from the United States), a youth hostel, and a synagogue, which would be the principal Reform synagogue in Israel.

We discussed fees and procedures, and we shook hands. In contrast to the inner voice which urged me to draw up a detailed contract when I first met the rabbis of Porat Yosef, in this case I had no such urge. In fact we have never signed a contract. Lawyers talk back and forth, construction proceeds, life goes on, and no contract has ever been finalized. Nor does anybody feel concern over its absence.

The more I considered the design for the Hebrew Union college, the more the idea of courtyards dominated my thoughts: I envisioned a sequence of spaces, public outdoor rooms intimately connected, contained by the buildings. One could walk through the complex from one section to another without a sense of going from one building to another. I did not want a group of buildings, but a singular fabric of many parts, like the Armenian Quarter.

The geography of the site inspired the design. The first courtyard, the principal entrance, would be at street level. Additional courtyards would then descend, following the topography one level at a time. The program called for separating pilgrims from the students on the campus. But I wondered how I could do this while allowing the pilgrims to experience the entire campus. I resolved the paradox by letting the courtyards serve the academic activities and the upper level arcades surrounding them (like mezzanines) serve the public activities.

On entering the complex, students and faculty would descend half a level into the principal ceremonial courtyard, then on into the library, classrooms, and so on. The public, coming for a visit, would go up half a level to the upper arcade, entering the reception building and continuing, as if on a sky-walk, looking down into the courtyards, to the synagogue at the other end. This way the public could view the academic life of the centre but a full storey would naturally separate the two activities.

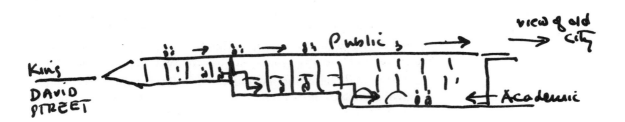

175

The courtyards were not the only outdoor space of the college. Towards the outer periphery I decided to create a series of walled gardens, each an echo or mirror of an interior room. Opposite the reading room in the library would be a reading garden. Each classroom would have a garden classroom next to it. To further merge the indoors and outdoors, I decided on large areas of glass. That led to a need for extra shading to cut down on the penetration of sun into the interior spaces during Jerusalem's hot summers. I decided to create a layer of trellises covered with plants, which in summer would create shade adjacent to all glass areas, but would let in the sunlight during winter.

That was in 1976. Four years were to pass before the Hebrew Union College finalized its agreement with the government and our work resumed.

Normally, there's never enough time to design. There is a kind of freshness and spontaneity to the buildings that happen that way. Habitat was one. The idea was there. It was drawn as it was built. There was no time to reflect.

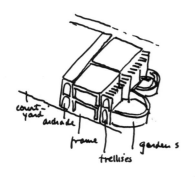

The Hebrew Union College was the opposite. I had the opportunity to reflect upon the plans and start to modify them in subtle ways, a little like good wine. Leave it long enough and that wine is going to get better.

For example, the first sketch contained the idea of the courtyards, the rooms, and the gardens, but the walls enclosing the gardens were all the same. The gardens were just a series of rectangular spaces, similar in size and character.

Upon reflection, I later concluded that while there was good reason for the concrete frame to repeat regularly throughout the building, there was no reason at all for the garden walls to repeat in the same way. Masonry is a malleable material, as Jefferson showed with his curved brick walls on the University of Virginia campus. You can shape walls, stiffen them and make them stronger by virtue of shape. I began to vary the walls, and this gave different gardens individual personalities.

The wall containing the reading-room garden became a semicircle, punctuated by a couple of mini-cylinders somewhat echoing Herod's plan of Herodion. I decided the walls containing the archaeological garden of the Museum would zigzag, following the property line except for one detour to clear three pine trees that had been preserved.

As the plans were submitted and approved, we were authorized to proceed with the construction documents. The love and care that had gone into the detailing of the Rau building, the original structure on the site, led me to be even more demanding than usual about the detailing of our own building. As Mies van der Rohe said, "God is in the details." And as I learned from Kahn, it is the integrity of the individual detail as part of the overall concept that can make or break a building.

How buildings age, their sense of timelessness or temporariness, has much to do with detailing. One wants to give a building longevity. It is not a quality to be taken for granted.

I have often found that contradictions in a program for a building become the source of richness. Just as the conflict between the academic and public life of the Hebrew Union complex gave birth to a two-level ciculation, so the conflict between the desire to build traditionally with stone on the one hand and in a contemporary fashion with modern materials on the other helped me to resolve the syntax or architectural language of the building.

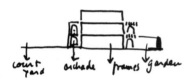

This development would not have been possible if I hadn't had the experience of designing and building Yeshivat Porat Yosef. In a sense, the design for the Hebrew Union College is in a direct path of evolution from the yeshiva: the idea of connecting past and present is manifested by juxtaposing, side by side, traditional and modern construction and having them play one against the other.

In the college I took these ideas further. In the yeshiva, concrete arches, modern in construction, mirrored the forms of the surrounding buildings. In the college, the concrete took the form of a frame of columns and beams as austere as a Japanese house, minimal in its utter simplicity. The frame is contained, surrounded, enclosed by the stone construction forming the arcades and garden walls. I felt that whether you walked inside or outside the buildings, you would experience simple framed spaces embellished by the sensuousness of the curved and arched stone walls. Studying the model in the office, I was struck by the fact that if I peeled away the curved garden walls and arches, I was left with the naked frame, which looked just like the frames of those Mies van der Rohe steel and glass buildings I felt to be so wanting. But juxtaposed, the contrasting forms resulted

177

in an experience neither traditional nor contemporary, something quite new.

We experimented with different mixes of concrete to find a hue harmonious with the deep yellow Jerusalem limestone walls. Ferrous oxide was added to give the concrete a travertine marble color.

In the 1976 sketches I had specified that the wall panels within the frame would be the machine-cut white stone veneer of the kind used in the existing Rau building. When yellow Jerusalem stone is cut by a saw, it comes out white. While this would match the panels of the original building there was something disturbing about the scale model when we inserted white sheets of paper to represent white stone. Instead of receding into the massive stone walls, these panels jumped out, becoming the dominant element.

I decided to experiment with a completely new material — aluminum. When aluminum foil replaced the white sheets in the model, at once something wonderful happened: the aluminum foil picked up the reflection of the yellow stone, and the panel surfaces receded, becoming calm and decorative. The silver and gold echoed the silver and gold domes of the shrines on the Temple Mount.

My colleagues in the office wondered if aluminum was not too high tech for Jerusalem. On the contrary, I argued, in the tradition of Mediterranean architecture, metal elements are often used together with masonry, bay window, and dome structures. Using aluminum would bring out the quality of the stone construction in contrast.

The next step was to present this to the client. Their reaction was reserved too. The building committee simply could not disassociate the material used here from that used in the Citicorp building in New York and other North American high-tech material buildings. They could not imagine how aluminum could coexist with the older materials.

They were also uncomfortable that aluminum was imported whereas stone veneer was local. Of course, many components in the building were imported — plumbing, air-conditioning components, and other fixtures, mostly invisible. But I was proposing the use of a high-tech western material on the visible facade of the building.

I was taking a risk and I knew it. I was going against all the conventions. Aluminum was convincing on the model, but would it work at full scale on the actual site? We were building a life size mock-up to test all materials. We could try it out. I immediately ordered two panels of aluminum (with windows to match) from Zimcor in Montreal.

When they arrived on site and a crew began to mount them, I hurried over. As soon as I saw the result, I knew that we had been right. The panels had a silvery glow to them and the reflection of sky and stone was wonderful. I immediately rushed to city hall and asked Amnon Niv, the city engineer, to come over and see the mock-up. He did, and reacted exactly as I had: on arriving he exclaimed, "That's just terrific. Just the right thing!"

With the city engineer's support, the city planning department at once approved our plans, including use of aluminum. A month later the approval was reversed by the District Committee, who questioned the suitability of the aluminum, not so much in my building, which they appreciated, but for the precedent it might set for other places.

I appealed the decision, and after further review of models and drawings, the aluminum was approved subject to one condition. As the District Planner explained, the use of aluminum constituted a violation of the city zoning ordinance and could be approved only if we put the plans on a ninety-day public deposition and public hearing period. This made the client nervous, as a public deposition might again call unwelcome attention to the project. Finally, because it would not delay construcion, they agreed. Four months later, after at least a dozen meetings with various community groups, including the Council for a Beautiful Israel and representatives of the Institute of Architects and Engineers, the aluminum panels were approved.

As we worked on the college I found myself in a new mood, a mood somewhat conditioned, I think, by the prevailing nervousness of contemporary architecture in and around Jerusalem. The new university campus on Mount Scopus, for example, zigzagged with nervous shapes and robust cantilevering, flexing its muscles. The new satellite towns had every conceivable shape piled one on top of the other. I found myself thirsting for calmness.

At that time we were completing the first sketches for the National Gallery of Canada, and I went on a rapid trip through Italy with Jean Sutherland Boggs, the chairman of the corporation charged with its building. We visited courtyards, arcades, colonnades, and grand stairs, ingredients which were to be in the Ottawa building and which we wanted to study. Time after time I rediscovered that those spaces which gave a sense of timelessness were severe in their simplicity. It was as if they had been allowed to simmer so that the trivia evaporated and only the essence remained.

I became obsessed with spaces that had a sense of calmness, where one was not distracted by the space, but experienced it as a setting. I wanted to create spaces that were not crying out: "I'm here, here's my architecture, see how clever I am," but where the architect is smiling, he's even winking; the architecture is there but it is your very own place.

Once again, it took a special client to be sensitive to these issues. Dick Scheuer would talk about the subtle play between cold and hot, silver and gold, or the plainness of a wall and its severity as it played off against the shadow pattern of the trellises, without pressing me to embellish it just because it was plain.

These are subtle matters, worthy of the time of a client and architect. When Rabbi Shrem asked, "Why don't you carve a candelabra on that blank stone wall?" I reacted (at least internally) with a sense of dismissal. But later I questioned that reaction. The desire to decorate is as old as the species: we paint our bodies, we make and wear jewellery, we build walls and embellish them. Why was it that I responded so negatively to the idea of carving a candelabra on a blank wall, and yet I could walk through a Gothic cathedral and enjoy the way each buttress was topped with a sculpted figure, or find pleasure in the layer upon layer of ornate carving over the arched entrance?

With a renewed interest in ornamentation and symbols, many architects now apply patterns and designs to the face of a building in exactly the same way the rabbi was asking me to carve the candelabra on the wall. Decoration as an appliqué is re-emerging.

I appreciate decoration in a building when it is integrated into the process of the decorating and the building. We take pleasure in a piece of lace; our enjoyment of its patterns is inseparable from our perception of the hands making it. Or take a Palestinian embroidered dress — our enjoyment derives in part from the colour and geometric patterns and the play between them, in part from the play between those patterns and the body of the woman who wears it, and in part in appreciating the toil and labor of its making.

Similarly our appreciation of an arabesque screen in a desert building stems not only from the rich geometric pattern but also from the subconscious awareness of the need for moving air through walls for proper ventilation.

The conical roof of the Temple of the Heavens in Peking is made of an interlocking pattern of log-shaped beams, with the ends of each log painted in a different colour — red, yellow, green, and the imprint of gold seals. When I am in that temple I sense that I have penetrated into a world of colour and pattern with deep roots in Chinese culture. Yet every element also reminds me of the ingenuity of the construction, the way the pieces interlock to form a strong, earthquake-proof structure. The colours and the gold seals are as much a celebration of that as the freestanding figure on top of the flying buttress in a Gothic cathedral — the saint who by his presence proclaims the very idea of a flying buttress, symbolically resisting the force of gravity that comes down from the vault, making an exclamation mark where the weight of the structure is being transmitted to the earth, the place also where the cathedral silhouette makes contact with the sky.

Symbols are sacred. A stained glass window represents ritual scenes that the master builder has integrated into the architecture. The window brings in bright light. The sunlight and the face of the Christ on the cross become one. When precisely the same image is painted on the wall, as it is in many baroque churches, it loses a measure of authenticity because instead of being integrated, it has become applied. It is removable. It feels thin. It becomes tentative. It has no space.

The college was inaugurated in November of 1986. It had become transformed from a project I had imagined and put on paper, into a place of working and living, enjoyed and appreciated in its reality. There is no greater reward for an architect.

RELIGIOUS ESTABLISHMENTS IN JUDAISM

There are three main streams in Judaism today: the Orthodox, the Conservative and the Reform Movements. The Orthodox includes both Sephardic and Ashkenazi Jews who practice Judaism by the Halacha (Talmudic interpretation of the Scriptures). These include the strictest observance of dietary laws and of the Sabbath (no active use of electricity, no driving or physical work of any kind).

The Conservative Movement, which emerged in the United States, has adopted some modifications — for example, men and women pray together in the synagogue chambers instead of being separated as in an Orthodox synagogue. There are more accommodations to the literal interpretation of the Halacha adapting to the realities of modern day life.

The Reform Movement emerged in Germany and spreading to the United States in the second half of the nineteenth century and introduced far reaching reforms in the interpretation of the Halacha and synagogue ritual. Reform worship is always with the men and women together; many men do not cover their heads during worship; observance of dietary laws is lax; conversion of Gentiles to Judaism, most often precipitated by mixed marriages, is accommodating and does not call for the rigorous (and what some may call humiliating) procedures of Orthodox conversion.

The great majority of Reform Jews live in the United States. Few Jews declare themselves Reform in Israel. Although only a minority of Israel's Jewish population actually practice Judaism under the rules of Orthodoxy, the majority consider themselves "nonpracticing" Orthodox Jews rather than Reform Jews. The conflict between the authority of Reform and Orthodox rabbis over Judaism, particularly in matters pertaining to conversion, has been the subject of a continuous parliamentary conflict in Israel which has come under the heading of "Who Is a Jew."

CHAPTER 17

THE COUNCIL OF THE TORAH SAGES

Through 1974 and 1975, Teddy Kollek continued to push my plan for the Western Wall. He felt that time was working against us. He believed that political developments in the world after the Yom Kippur War guaranteed that any action by Israel in Jerusalem would be subject to criticism, particularly in the United Nations. The announcement of a plan for the Western Wall precinct would focus the criticism even more sharply but the longer we waited the less able Israel would be to withstand the criticism.

It was just at that time that UNESCO, dominated by the Arab bloc and supported by third world country votes, began to condemn Israel for changing the face and the image of Jerusalem. Many Israelis have a semi-paranoid attitude to U.N. organizations — "the whole world is against us; we must stand on our own" — and I must say, after the UNESCO attacks, I could understand them. In 1948 UNESCO had not said one word against the destruction of all holy places in the Jewish Quarter after Jordan took possession of Jerusalem; it did not pass any resolutions when roads were built through the Jewish cemetery on the Mount of Olives; it did not object when the crest of the Mount of Olives was desecrated by the Inter-Continental Hotel.

But after Israel reunited the city, UNESCO criticized archaeological excavations which displaced no one and uncovered important structures, increasing our knowledge of the history of Jerusalem, including its Muslim periods. There was certainly no attempt to erase that Muslim presence once it had been uncovered.

Soon after the Rabin government was installed, the Mayor arranged for a review of the Western Wall plans by the new Prime Minister. After a presentation to Rabin, which took place in the same room as that meeting with Golda Meir, we gained his approval and authorization to formally present the scheme to the Cabinet Committee for Jerusalem.

Rabin's Minister of Justice, Haim Zadok, operated very differently from his predecessor, Ya'acov Shimshon Shapira. Where Shapira deferred to Golda Meir, Zadok was forceful and wanted to run his own show. His appearance was similarly forceful. He had grizzled, greying hair which stood almost vertically, a receding forehead, and owl-like eyes. Not only was he a Minister of Justice, but by a fluke of Israeli coalition politics, he was, at that same time, the Minister of Religious Affairs. The timeless coalition between the Labour party and the religious parties for the first time had been disrupted.

Every Labour government since 1948 had included the religious parties. This was a small price to pay for a majority in the Knesset: the religious parties gave their support on economic and foreign issues, in return for Labour's support on religious matters. Until the Rabin government, there had never been a Minister of Religious Affairs who was not a member of the National Religious Party (NRP). But when Rabin was unable to come to an agreement that would bring the NRP into his coalition, he appointed Zadok to the religious portfolio. For the time being, therefore, I did not have to deal with the religious establishment. It proved to be a moment we paid for dearly. I was to become identified as the architect that Zadok tried to push through at the time of this estrangement. Those few months during which the religious establishment was excluded from discussions about the Western Wall forever alienated them from my plan.

At the national level, the price was, of course, much higher. With the permanent coalition disrupted, the religious parties turned to the right. In the next election, they joined forces to form the government with Likkud and Begin. Undoubtedly, this shift to the right not only represented their disappointment at what they sensed as a betrayal, but also symbolized the emergence of ultra-nationalistic right wing sentiments within the religious establishment. This made the partnership with Likkud more meaningful to them.

Standing in the room that day with the Cabinet Committee for Jerusalem, I could only be delighted by the fact that there was one less minister to deal with.

The opposition to the Western Wall plan was developing on two levels. One was political, arising from the battle over jurisdiction of the area and not design concerns. It emerged from the suspicions that the city commissioned me in order to dislodge the religious groups who had control of the Wall. That was enough to stir up the religious factions.

I had worked closely with the official architect of the Ministry of Religious Affairs. I had integrated his material, compiled over the years, into our work. But the Minister, the Company for the Reconstruction and Development of the Jewish Quarter, and the Mayor could not agree on a modus operandi and hence were unable to sign the tripartite agreement that had been drawn up in early 1973. The differences between the parties were almost too subtle to understand. The Minister of Religious Affairs was concerned that signing this agreement might relinquish his ministry's control over the area. No amount of reassurance from Teddy could persuade him otherwise.

The second set of objections arose from the architectural community. Why should Safdie be given the commission for the Wall? What was the review process that led to his appointment? Why not have a competition?

The Cabinet Committee, aware of the many conflicts, decided that the matter should be studied by a commission, made up of independent architects and several officials, which would hold public hearings. They appointed as chairman the new head of the Company for the Reconstruction and Development of the Jewish Quarter, Erwin Shimron, an attorney. The commission came to be called the Shimron Commission. (When he later headed a commission on organized crime by the same name, it made for some mischievous misunderstandings.)

Our Shimron Commission was made up of three architects appointed by the architectural association, Yaacov Rechter, Arieh Sharon, and Avraham Yaski; the Deputy Mayor, Meron Benvenisti; the representative of the archaeological community, Meir Ben-Dov; a representative of the Ministry of Religious Affairs, David Cassuto; and Yehuda Tamir, the ex-chairman of the Company for the Reconstruction and Development of the Jewish Quarter, as an observer.

Meanwhile a seemingly unimportant event occurred whose dramatic consequences were to emerge only later. My friend Bruno Zevi wanted to publish the plan for the Wall in his magazine *L'Architectura* and had asked David Fisher, a young Israeli architect who was studying in Florence, to collect drawings, photographs, and program information. Fisher spent several days in my office gathering material before going back to his studies in Italy.

My first meeting with the Shimron Commission took place in the Jewish Quarter in a restored room with a vaulted stucco ceiling. Small windows looked towards the Mount of Olives. The members of the commission sat around a large U-shaped table in the centre, with the visiting experts or witnesses at the open end.

I expected David Cassuto, the Ministry of Religious Affairs' representative, to be a large, substantial Italian, but to my surprise he was a short, very thin person, almost fragile, with hollow cheeks, thin lips, and light narrow blue eyes. Clean shaven, wearing a skullcap, he was a man fitting Shakespeare's description of Cassius, a man with a lean and hungry look.

It took me fifteen seconds to learn how his mind worked. Before he'd taken more than a superficial look at the model, he interrupted me with a prepared, party-line speech about how the religious community had very particular needs that must be the subject of an intensive programmatic study. He went on to proclaim that only people from the religious community could define these needs. He proposed another commission made up of wise men, rabbis, experts from the rabbinate and other scholars of appropriate credibility. Out of their deliberations, a program might emerge. The present committee, he rasped, did not know what they were talking about.

Needless to say, this didn't sit well with the other commission members. Benvenisti, a seasoned politician, dismissed Cassuto as somebody who was playing a tape of the party line. Meir Ben-Dov kept needling him with the usual antagonism archaeologists have for the religious establishment who question their right to dig. He also expressed his own secular resentment of attempts by the religious minority to impose their views on the entire Israeli society.

On the whole, though, I enjoyed the hearings. Shimron invited some of the great minds of the country — men like Professor Joshua Prawer (an expert on the Crusader period and Christian history) and several fine scholars of Jewish history such as archaeologist Yigael Yadin. They responded with their vision of Jerusalem and its significance in the life of the nation. At these times, I found the meetings very constructive and illuminating. This discourse helped me to strengthen the design.

Finally, after seven long months of discussion, the commission recommended my plan as the basis for future action. There were, however, two issues to be rethought. The commission was not convinced that the buildings on the cliff overlooking the Wall should be demolished, nor that the cliff should be hidden by new construction. They wanted that feature reviewed.

Their final recommendation was, I suppose, predictable, but to me somewhat enervating. They proposed yet another steering committee, consisting of public figures from the fields of architecture, history, and religion who would work with me on the revision of the plan before it went to the municipal planning authority. After all, even with national blessing, planning approval is under the jurisdiction of the city.

The Shimron Commission concluded its investigation and sent its report to the cabinet for further action on May 17, 1977, exactly four days before the elections.

Rabin's Labour government fell, taking with it the Cabinet Committee which had approved the plan. Menachem Begin's Likkud party took over and formed a new government.

It seemed my fate to be involved in projects which required longevity or, more critically, staying power. Having met, discussed, presented, explained, and cultivated the various ministers in question and the members of the Shimron Commission, I was now faced with a whole group of new actors totally ignorant of the subject. It was a scenario I was to relive many times in future years — when I was building the National Gallery in Ottawa and the Museum for Quebec, federal and provincial governments changed mid-stream. The only constant in Jerusalem was Teddy. Governments came and went, but Teddy was there, one hoped, forever.

It was just at this moment that David Fisher reappeared. He had written a critical piece in *L'Architectura*, calling my plan inadequate. I'm used to bad reviews, and it didn't bother me much. My real surprise came when he returned to Jerusalem with a model of an alternative plan that he had prepared for the Wall.

Fisher, "religious" himself, had the active support of David Cassuto. With the help of his religious friends, he peddled his plan in the Knesset and then put it on exhibition in a hall in the Old City. He invited journalists and promoted the plan as an alternative that met the needs of the religious community.

He proposed a large platform, not unlike Noguchi's, at the level where people pray today. Below it, he planned a whole series of caverns and excavated spaces where archaeological remains would be hidden. I found the design amateurish.

Begin's new government had established an entirely new Cabinet committee on Jerusalem. The decision made by the previous committee now required the approval of the new committee. The Mayor was, as always, my willing ally in pushing my plan forward.

But this new committee seemed paralyzed; they had problems handling the simplest issues, let alone the Wall. The Mayor became exasperated and soon refused to attend their meetings or take further initiatives, saying there was no chance of getting anywhere with the Begin government. He wanted to wait and conserve our energy.

I could not be so stoic. I was becoming increasingly irritated with the distortions of Fisher, Cassuto and company. I was determined to pursue the project further.

In the hope of overcoming the religious opposition, I initiated a meeting with the two chief rabbis. Both Chief Rabbi Shlomo Goren and Chief Rabbi Ovadia Yosef had seen the plan in 1974 and made favorable public statements at the time. Both received me again: Goren expressed general approval, and Ovadia Yosef said that while he was favorably disposed I had to appreciate that a matter of this significance required the approval of the highest council of the rabbinate. He offered to convene it.

My meeting with the Chief Rabbinical Council took place in the chief rabbinate building on King George V Street, a somewhat pompous cube-shaped building with massive stone piers topped with a stone dome. Though it had been built in the fifties, the detailing had touches of Mussolini's monumental architecture, the vocabulary of the thirties. The meeting room, with its plain white ceiling and white walls, was the antithesis of the exterior. Three or four tables were arranged in an oval. Rabbi Zolti had a long wispy white beard, white hair, and burning blue eyes. Rabbi Ovadia Yosef wore the formal dress, with the black onion-shaped hat, of the Sephardic Chief Rabbi, and his beard, moustache, and eyes were all coal black. All the rabbis were bearded and dressed in black. The scene looked like a Rembrandt etching come to life. Out of respect for the sages, I wore a Kipah (skullcap).

I began with a description of the plan and the central issues it tried to address. The setting immediately affected my language. I began to do something I never do ordinarily when speaking Hebrew — addressing people in the third person. It is an old-fashioned way of showing respect, and I found myself saying not "you" but "he" and "His Honour."

About half the discussion with the Council had to do with concepts, and with questions of ritual. But another part of the discussion had to do with practicalities and with politics.

Ovadia Yosef turned to me and said, "You know, Mr. Safdié" (he always spoke my name with the Sephardic pronunciation, accenting the é) "the most important thing for us to protect and preserve is the ability of our people to pray by this most holy place, so that it be not abandoned for a single moment. Any action or construction that would disrupt those prayers for even one minute would prevent us from approving the plan."

I was ready for this. "We have met with experts in the field," I said, "and have devised a plan: a temporary structure of wood planks supported on metal struts, as is done when subways are constructed, would allow the praying to go on while the excavation goes on beneath. Only when everything is completed, not for many years, would we dismantle the structure and transform the area. Archaeological excavation is a very quiet process; it's really a hand operation. We are not blasting the rock, we are just removing fill. That would not disrupt the praying."

But that led immediately to the political question: "You know we have no trust in the archaeologists." He went on passionately, "They have misled us, they have prevented us from praying at the south side of the Western Wall itself. Who knows what shall come to pass? What if they find a mosque? What if they find an important church? What if they decide they've unearthed some important archaeological discovery that must at all costs be preserved? What about our access to our Wall then? We do not trust them."

I tried to soften the atmosphere. "Maybe they will uncover the Menorah." (the great candelabra of the Temple which had been lost). But there were no smiles . . . I went on, "I've discussed the matter with the Mayor. He shares your conviction that there, prayers should have precedence. He even recommended that a treaty be drawn up and signed by the city, the Chief Rabbis, the Department of Antiquities, the archaeologists, the Ministry of Religious Affairs, and the Ministry of Justice, which would declare that no matter what was found above the Herodian Street, it would be removed. It might be documented and photographed first but it would be removed."

Chief Rabbi Yosef smiled and addressed me in an almost fatherly way. I was a member of his community, an Aleppo Jew. "We trust you," he said. "We would trust also any agreement reached with you. But this is a complicated and unpredictable world. These agreements have ways of being broken. Treaties between man and man — and not only those, but treaties between governments and organizations — have ways of being circumvented."

All I could do was repeat my belief in the sincerity of the parties. And he replied, "Yes, I believe in the sincerity of Teddy Kollek too. But who knows who shall be the Mayor of Jerusalem five years hence?" I'd already presented the plan to two Prime Ministers and was about to deal with a third, so I had to acknowledge the wisdom of his skepticism.

I expressed my conviction that nothing around the Wall should be of such a mass or importance as to overshadow it. I introduced the idea of gradually building up the terraces from bedrock and letting the buildings which face the Wall almost merge into the landscape. I wanted the solid mass of the Wall to be the strong presence and the rest of the site to focus attention toward it.

Rabbi Zolti leaned forward with a friendly twinkle and said, "You know, the Wall is not the Temple. Do you not find something almost appropriate about its temporary look? It is, after all, only the remnant of the Temple. We do believe in the rebuilding of the Third Temple, and we must not make the design feel and appear too complete or final."

Although this concept of incompleteness and impermanence had been in my head while I was working on the design, I now realized, as we looked at the model, that it did have something too final about it because it showed every detail. I knew as an architect that it would never work out that way. It would take years to implement the plan. The realities of life and the site would intervene in the design and change the details. But I had not found a way to physically present that in a model.

I said, "His Honour is right. This design is too complete and final. But beware of misreading its intention. It weaves together the remnant of the Second Temple, the streets upon which our ancestors walked toward the Temple, and whatever insitutions it must accommodate." But I realized that saying it and demonstrating it were not the same thing. At that moment a seed was planted in my mind for a new approach.

I had to rethink the plan, giving much more presence and significance to some of the existing components on the site. I had to find a new method of communicating the plan if the design for the Western Wall precinct were ever to become a reality in my lifetime.

THE WAR OF THE WORDS

"THE SPIRIT OF SAFDIE HOVERS OVER THE WESTERN WALL!" Nadav Shragai wrote in *Ha'aretz* in September 1985:

"With the precision of a Swiss watch, an excitement comes upon Jerusalem every year before the High Holidays — stormy correspondence between the municipality of Jerusalem, the Ministry of Religious Affairs and the Company for the Reconstruction and Development of the Jewish Quarter. The first volleys are fired by this triumvirate when anyone dares to consider moving even a single stone in the precinct of the Western Wall. At that point, the struggle becomes public. Functionaries and politicians have changed with the years — they come and go — but they wave the same flags — now faded from overuse. The pattern is consistant. The conflict surrounds the small parcel of land dear to the Jewish nation, the Western Wall precinct, the remnant of our temple.

"The focus upon which the Ministry of Religious Affairs concentrates is the plan of the architect Moshe Safdie, which if it did not exist would have had to be invented by the Ministry. Each time that anyone sneezes too loudly around the Western Wall precinct, the Ministry bureaucrats jump and scream, 'This is a Safdie plan being sneaked in through the back door.' Sometimes there is truth to their claims.

"If the Safdie plan *had* become reality, undoubtedly many would have recommended giving the talented architect the Israel Prize in one of our forthcoming Independence Days . . .

"Safdie, according to his supporters, has exceptional vision, rare talent and the soul of an artist. His opponents term his attributes as excessive imagination and megalomania . . .

"Each time that the district committee discusses improvements to the area, the Ministry of Religious Affairs opposes it, claiming no one consulted them. The municipality claims that the precinct is not under the jurisdiction of the Ministry of Religious Affairs. The ministry produces a map, dated January 11, 1972, signed by the Minister of Justice and Religious Affairs. The maps show the precinct in front of the Wall designated to the jurisdiction of the ministry. The municipality, in turn, produces a legal opinion arguing that this jurisdiction is limited to matters of keeping the Sabbath, monitoring appropriate dress and controlling commercial activity. The Ministry of Religious Affairs has its own legal advisor who interprets the law differently . . . And so the discussion continues."

CHAPTER 18

HOLOCAUST MEMORIAL

In 1976, I received a call from Dr. Izhak Arad, director of the Yad Vashem Holocaust Memorial Museum in Jerusalem. I had been to Yad Vashem several times. My initial visit was an experience of profound shock, bewilderment, and disbelief. Although my first wife was a Holocaust survivor, the visual documentation of the Holocaust was beyond my comprehension. On subsequent visits, I have always had to bring someone with me. One becomes a standing witness to the other person's initiation to horror.

Dr. Arad asked me to meet with him that day at Yad Vashem. As we left the museum, he proceeded to a small hill located between the museum and the administrative building, which overlooked the mountains of Judea. Arad explained that there was nothing in the museum dedicated to the million and a half children who had perished in the Holocaust. As he spoke, I thought of the shoes of a young baby found in one of the camps, copied and cast into metal and placed in a glass box. For me, those small shoes were more powerful and disturbing than the explicit photographs of mass graves and decomposed bodies. He asked whether I would accept a commission to design a museum devoted and dedicated to the children of the

Holocaust. I was surprised and moved that he and his colleagues would consider me to be the right architect.

He explained that their archives were rich with material. There were drawings and paintings done by children in the camps, along with their clothing, letters, and photographs. "Let me spend some time examining the material and considering the kind of museum I might build on this hill," I suggested.

I returned to Jerusalem four weeks later, having cleared my schedule for several days. I spent hour after hour in the archives, increasingly depressed by what I saw. I began to feel saturated. Then I realized that everyone who would be coming to the Children's Memorial would be arriving from the main structure, having been immersed in the horrific experience through photographs, films and objects. After this exposure, could they absorb still more? Rather than providing yet more documentation, this Children's Memorial should be a place to pause and reflect, to meditate, after the visit to the main museum. I wanted to create a place of memory and contemplation. I wanted to focus upon the lives and souls of the dead children. A natural stone archway led to the site, protruding from the bedrock. I thought of building a ramp under the arch which would lead to an underground room. Here, there would be total darkness and a single memorial candle. One would leave the room on the opposite side, heading toward the north, emerging from the hill to overlook the mountains and the forest. This would represent a return to life and an optimistic future. But the single candle in the underground chamber might be oppressive. Its singularity seemed inappropriate to the millions of souls. I began wondering how the one candle might be multiplied. I wanted it to float in space, to float into infinity. I envisioned a space expanded rather than limited to that which radiates from a single candle.

I recalled the exhibition Labyrinth at Expo '67, a National Film Board exhibit designed by Colin Low, Roman Kroiter, Wolf Koenig and other friends of mine. Leading to the theatres was a bridgeway suspended between semi-reflected glass sheets. The double/triple/quadruple reflections of a few light sources suspended between the sheets multiplied into infinity and created a festive procession. If similar sheets of glass were arranged around a candle and around the walls of a room, they might multiply by reflection, a single memorial candle into millions of flames extending into infinity. One would be in a room surrounded in all directions by flames of the memorial candle, the souls of the children.

I called Colin Low and asked him if my idea would work. What kind of glass did they use? How did the reflections work? We agreed to collaborate. Glass was ordered from the same manufacturer to make a model.

We decided to make a model large enough to stick one's head into. We speculated that if the candle were surrounded by three panels of glass, forming a triangle; if the triangle were surrounded by six panels forming a hexagon; and if the outer walls, ceiling and floor of the room were lined with mirrors, then a single light source would be multiplied into infinity. We constructed the model. Peering through a small aperture we watched as the candle was inserted.

It was like a miracle. As if thrown into space, floating between galaxies, each twitch in movement of the flame multiplied to the right, to the left — a strange dance of the souls. At once I was convinced of the power of the experience to stop one's routine thoughts and make one pause and remember.

The entrance area was similarly designed, but instead of the candles there would be three photographs of the eyes of children in the camps, again multiplied many times, floating into space.

With considerable excitement I presented the model in Jerusalem to Arad and his committee. First there was the shock of surprise at the unexpected. They were so conditioned to think in terms of objects, exhibits and documentation, that the counter-idea, the place to remember, caught them unprepared. I left the meeting uncertain of their response. They wanted to consult others. They had no sense of how people would react. Arad called a week later. He had shown it to members of his board and some members of the Knesset. Each had bent over and inserted his head in the aperture in the model. Time and time again people were moved — some, to tears. But the air of uncertainty remained. "We would like to proceed," he said, "but first we must raise the money."

In 1978 when I left for Cambridge, Massachusetts, I said good-bye to Colin Low in Montreal. Both of us had assumed the project was dormant. Either funds were not available or perhaps the will was not there.

Six years later, in 1984, Arad phoned once again. Abraham Spiegel of Los Angeles had seen the model. A camp survivor himself, Spiegel had lost his two-year-old son in Auschwitz. "He wants to build it," Arad said.

And so the tractors moved in and excavated the hill. The rock was carefully carved, the roof-slab constructed, and cypress trees were planted on top. Special glass was ordered from Holland. On June 28, 1987 the president of Israel opened the memorial in a public ceremony. Abraham Spiegel, his wife, and two of his children born after the war were present. It was a brilliantly sunny day and hundreds of guests listened to the speeches. And then, as the ribbon was cut, they descended down the ramp into the darkness.

Mrs. Spiegel had not seen the memorial under construction. I guided her into the place of infinite candles. I cried as she cried.

CHAPTER 19

HARVARD COMES TO JERUSALEM

As work was proceeding on Mamilla and on the renovation of the Jewish Quarter and the satellite towns, I became increasingly anxious about the lack of attention given pivotal sites linking the Arab and Israeli districts. Damascus Gate was being ignored, along with the large vacant piece of land stretching northward from it toward the American Colony Hotel and Mount Scopus. I felt it was urgent to have these and other sensitive areas carefully studied.

It was at that time, 1978, that I moved to Cambridge and became director of Urban Design at Harvard. During my first year there, we studied the Montreal waterfront. By the end of the year, I realized how useful the study had been to the City of Montreal. It had opened the eyes of both city officials and the public to many unconsidered possibilities. This gave me an idea: on the one hand I had Harvard students and faculty in search of a laboratory for meaningful study; on the other, a rapidly developing Jerusalem was in need of talent and energy to study its many urban design facets. Putting the two together might help solve both problems.

But Jerusalem was not a bus ride away from Cambridge as Montreal was. The logistics and cost of getting students and faculty to Israel and immersing them in the city were somewhat overwhelming. Hundreds of thousands of dollars would be required.

I had never raised funds before; I always found the process somewhat humiliating. After two not very successful attempts at support in Boston and California, Teddy Kollek directed me to Irving Schneider, one of the principals of Helmsley Spear in New York, as someone who could help identify potential sponsors. Schneider's daughter, Lynn, was a graduate in architecture from Harvard and had worked in my office.

I spoke with Schneider and he agreed to meet with me. Before discussing the financial considerations, I emphasized the importance of this project to the future of Jerusalem. There were many voices in Jerusalem that had to be heard in the planning process: the voices of the Arab minority, Muslim and Christian groups, as well as diverse Jewish religious movements. The proposed study would create a setting in which these community groups would really be listened to. Not only would they want to identify their needs, but they would shed their paranoid protective coats. After I outlined the costs that were involved, Irving Schneider responded with the promise of support. "No need to go seeking sponsors," he said. "I'll do it myself."

The response from Harvard was not unanimously favorable when I first proposed the project. Some members of the faculty were afraid that Harvard's involvement would be a tacit support of Israel's claim to Jerusalem or that it might not be the impartial study of the city that met the needs of both the Jewish and Arab communities.

The matter was reviewed by the appropriate authorities at the university. My brief pointed out we would focus only on design and social problems and avoid the issue of sovereignty. The students would meet members of the Israeli as well as Arab communities, and the visiting lecturers and guest critics at Harvard would include Muslims, Christians, and Jews.

Their answer came back: accepted.

We were off. The first group of forty students arrived in September 1980. We surveyed the city within the walls, we went to the Holy Sepulchre and the Temple Mount, we visited Hezekiah's pool and the Tombs of the Kings. We also took bus trips to the suburbs; we explored every part of the city. We studied the Old City, the Damascus and Lions Gate areas, and the processional route from the Mount of Olives along the Via Dolorosa, as well as the suburban development of northern and southern Jerusalem and the revitalization of downtown Jerusalem and the entrances to the city. The students also heard a series of lectures and met leading members of the Arab and Israeli communities; they heard engineers, architects, historians, archaeologists; they even met poets, like Yehuda Amichai, who read his passionate poems on Jerusalem.

In the three years of the studies, some 250 students came to Jerusalem in eight groups, working with seven faculty members.

An important move was to enlist the aid of Nader Ardalan, who was a member of the Aga Khan Muslim Architecture Committee. Nader and his students decided to focus on the Old City, particularly the Muslim Quarter and the major religious processional routes into the Old City.

The Waqf, the Muslim Religious Council, administered the Muslim holy places, which included the Haram esh-Sharif, the Temple Mount. It also owned most of the buildings in the Muslim Quarter, which it leased out to residents. In order to make a meaningful study of the Muslim Quarter, we had to make contact with them — not an easy proposition. But Nader's connections made it possible. The students met Arab families living in the Muslim Quarter, surveyed their living conditions, and then developed proposals for the rehabilitation of the Bab el Huta area, the worst slum in Jerusalem.

Ardalan began developing interesting ideas with his group. I felt he should meet the Mayor and invited him for dinner on an evening when the Mayor could come. Teddy Kollek had a community meeting first, and we were already into the cheeses when he arrived.

He joined us on our terrace overlooking the Western Wall. He helped himself to wine and cheese and listened as we talked of the deplorable conditions in the Muslim Quarter. The Waqf constantly rejected the municipality's attempts to fund renovation programs in the Muslim Quarter, imagining them to be Machiavellian schemes for driving Muslims from the Quarter. Whenever the municipality talked about room crowding and excessive density, the Waqf interpreted that as an intent to reduce the Arab population within the city walls.

I thought Teddy was dozing, but he suddenly turned to Nader. "If you can get the Jordanians and the Waqf to cooperate with you in embarking on a restoration program in the Muslim Quarter, you will have my complete support."

I sat up. "You mean, if they agree to initiate a rehabilitation program with Ardalan as their architect and urban designer, the municipality would back the effort?"

He nodded. "We could easily have expropriated these properties and initiated rehabilitation. But for political reasons we haven't because it would always be misinterpreted as an attempt to dispossess them. But if you can get their cooperation . . . "

Nader went on a fund-raising trip through Saudi Arabia, Kuwait, Jordan, and Morocco, armed with a letter from the Mayor. The Mayor had also briefed the Foreign Ministry on his commitment, to make sure they would back the project when the time came.

Nader encountered scepticism at first, but then he met with the Crown Prince of Jordan, who proved receptive. A small committee was formed to review Nader's proposal, which he elaborated into a ten-year plan.

One day Nader called me from Paris and announced that sufficient funds were now appropriated for the field surveys. Needless to say, I was delighted. Preliminary work was started by Ardalan only to be brought to a halt with the regional tensions caused by the outbreak of the Lebanon War.

After three years of intensive work, the eight groups produced 150 plans. The more interesting projects were covered in a book entitled *The Harvard Jerusalem Studio*.

But publications were not my primary interest. My main concern was Damascus Gate. The gate was the principal service entrance into the Old City. Almost by default, the large empty triangle outside the gate had come to accommodate all the services and facilities required by the Old City. Crowded together were a sherut (communal) taxi stand serving all the villages of the West Bank, a major bus terminal close to the Garden Tomb, makeshift seasonal markets for melons and other fruit, an unloading section for goods — with thirty or forty trucks parked at any given time — and always lots of porters with carts waiting to carry goods in and out of the old city. Recent excavation at the gate itself had uncovered the original Roman Gate under the Ottoman one, which naturally attracted more tourists. And on holidays, all kinds of vendors lined the steps outside the gate.

The students had generated several exciting designs for the area and, coincidentally, an event had taken place that indicated the area was ripe for development.

Influential Protestant groups were upset with the constant roar of bus engines and clouds of exhaust pumping into the Garden Tomb from the adjacent Arab bus station. They were prepared to raise up to twelve million dollars to rectify the situation. The city engineer's office prepared plans to relocate the station and thus make it possible to landscape the area around the tomb.

I heard about the design from the Mayor and asked Amnon Niv to show it to me. It was depressingly dull. Almost any one of our students' plans would have been better. Of course, these had been created in a vacuum innocent of the practical problems that had to be resolved — transportation, land ownership, phasing, and so on.

Here was one of the most sensitive areas of Jerusalem, perhaps more important than Mamilla to the future life of the city. Was it going to be resolved on the basis of a makeshift plan done with the limited attention and resources in the city engineer's office?

How, I wondered, could we harness the energy and talent of the Harvard students to improve the planning?

One Friday evening Michal and I went down to the Damascus Gate for a walk. Across from the Gate on the vacant land along the Street of the Prophets, merchants put up temporary stalls to sell watermelons. We discovered that a large shed had been built alongside the city wall. As darkness fell, floodlights lit the city wall and the gate, and the melon shed became a glowing birthday cake, illuminated with strings of incandescent lamps and fluorescent tubes attached to its fragile wood columns.

Loud music broke Jerusalem's customary evening silence, and the smell of roasting meats filled the air. We crossed to the shed. It had been built out of small pieces of timber. The roof was stretched burlap (only Jerusalem with its guaranteed rainless summer allowed that). Tables of various sizes were set on loose gravel, each was packed, with hardly a chair to be found. The back of the shed was covered with mirrors that doubled the apparent size and also reflected the illuminated city wall. A dozen or so young Arab men were rushing from table to table carrying trays with mint tea, Turkish coffee, watermelon, and pita bread filled with meats.

We went in and saw an enormous steaming samovar sitting on a long counter in the centre along with several large baskets of fresh mint leaves for tea. Behind the table several men prepared the food. At the other end of the shed, a dozen charcoal grills were covered with skewers of meat. Strung along the ceiling from column to column, mingled with strings of lights, were strips of flags celebrating Coca-Cola, Sprite, and Schweppes. Near the entrance stood a scruffy looking man, his face unshaven, his belted pants slipping below his large pot belly, screaming at the top of his voice in Arabic: "Ahmed, table number three, see what they need! Hassan, on the double, hurry up, two beers to table four! Muhammed, get off your ass, seat those people at the corner table. Faster, faster!"

Michal and I sat on straw chairs at a small table — a slab of thin plywood covered with Formica — four wrought iron legs sinking in the gravel. At each corner of the room was a large television screen broadcasting Michael Jackson. As we sat, Michal gave me a knowing look. We had both noticed something very unusual for Jerusalem. The room was filled with both Palestinians and Israelis. To our right was a group of some twenty young Arabs, one holding a drum. As he beat it they all clapped hands and sang a rhythmic song. The singing did not prevent the teenage Israelis from following Jackson on the screen nor did it disturb the groups of middle-aged adults engaged in their serious discussions.

Several young men appeared at the entrance seeking a table. "Are they Israelis or Arabs?" I asked Michal. They sat not far from us and we heard them speak Hebrew. They were soldiers on leave.

And so there by the Damascus Gate, the people of the city came together. They did not mix at the tables, but they were sharing the same living space. Where the inaction and bureaucracy of the politicians and the planning authorities had failed, an enterprising café owner in a makeshift building sensed where the right spot was and brought the people of Jerusalem together.

Somehow we had to get our graduates to develop a scheme for the area, to create an opportunity for development. In search of financing, I went back to Schneider. I was hoping he would fund a group of graduates who would make a real plan for the area and, to my pleasure, he agreed to support a fourth year — a fellowship. We would choose three outstanding graduates who had worked on the Jerusalem studies and send them with a salary and all expenses paid for a one-year fellowship under Harvard auspices. Working as independent fellow with the full cooperation of the city engineers and transportation planners, they would design a plan for the Damascus

Gate area that would meet the practical requirements and provide a basis for development.

Three talented graduates were chosen: Gene Dyer, a graduate in urban design; Clifton Page, a graduate in architecture; and Ted Johnson, a graduate in landscape architecture.

It did not take them long to develop credibility in the city. Amnon Niv spent a half day weekly with them and the transportation planners thought of them almost as an extension of their own office. A faculty committee travelled to Jerusalem about every six weeks to review their work, and they returned twice to Cambridge to present it to the faculty and the students, for comments and advice.

A basic aspect of the concept was to integrate Israeli and Arab buses in a new terminal, thus creating a setting for interaction and mixing of the population. Some of the questions were: How big a bus station? How many buses? Where do they go? What kind of interchanges? Should the Arab and Israeli bus lines share facilities? The Israeli bus system consisted of a single company, Egged, but the Arab system comprised a dozen or more companies, many of them single line companies running a service for one village.

The fellows had difficulty getting information from the bus companies in eastern Jerusalem, so they turned to the municipal transportation planning office, who said they would be delighted to help but would take three months to get approval for a study and six months to make the surveys. The answers would be available just about a week before the students went back to Cambridge.

The problem was overcome, they proudly reported to us when we arrived for the faculty review, by initiating a series of personal surveys. They rode all the buses, a few days on one line and a few days on another. By making note of where people got off, asking them about their destinations, they had, within a few weeks, more information on the Arab bus lines than the municipal transportation office had.

At the end of the year, their work was summarized in a series of very fine drawings and a model outlining a multiphase plan for the area. Amnon Niv endorsed it enthusiastically and recommended that their plan be the basis of a submission to the municipal planning authorities. Before the students left, the Jerusalem Foundation and the municipality gave their approval and submitted the plan to the District Committee for approval.

This brought the Harvard study program full circle, from an academic exercise of benefit to Jerusalem, Harvard and obviously the students themselves to a tangible product that would have an impact on the future of the city.

In 1985, the fellows received the *Progressive Architecture* first Urban Design award for their plan.

CHAPTER 20

RETHINKING THE GRAND SCHEME

One day in 1980 while we were busy working on the Hebrew Union College, a phone call came from the chairman of ARIM — yet another government development corporation. I was surprised to learn that the ministry had decided, after many years, that it was time to turn over Manchat for development to ARIM.

"I understand that you were given planning approval years ago on the Manchat site," the chairman of ARIM said. "Rarely do we find in Jerusalem a parcel of land that already has approved plans. What would you think about proceeding with your designs for Manchat?"

I had not even glanced at the plans since 1976 but I was certainly still interested. As I hung up the phone, I asked that plans be brought up from the vaults in the basement. I hoped the mice hadn't eaten them.

When the drawings were finally located, I pulled them out of their encasements. Having been stored so long in our un-air-conditioned Jerusalem office, they showed their age. The paper was yellowed around the edges and almost brittle. We pinned them up.

There was a long silence.

I could see in my mind's eye the image of an enormous construction site with sixteen cranes running back and forth, lifting the huge elements into place, creating shelter for all the families who would come to live there . . . It seemed anachronistic, that image of an instant city, predetermining the form of a community with such finality. Why seal the lives of a thousand families — diverse as they would be, young and old, eastern and western — into a preconceived variety of apartments?

For all of the variety we had boasted about — small and large units, split level units, one storey duplexes — in the end there was a sameness about all the apartments. The place had the "project" look.

For years I had been saying that the central problem in designing a housing project was to overcome the project look. Now, I thought, I have created the project look myself.

I remembered driving around the suburbs of Jerusalem with the Harvard students and seeing the looks on their faces as we entered a "project town." Here was this great cluster of buildings, separated by highways and wide roads. We confronted endless rows of apartments like the suburbs of so many European cities, all brand new. In spite of the varied designs the many architects had attempted for new towns, one could not escape the project look. There was this same sense of uniformity in my 1967 design. In 1967 there was a particular notion of the role of the architect. The architect designed the environment completely, down to the last detail. He designed the house, the closets, the indirect lighting in the closets, the fiberglass bathrooms, the efficient kitchens. He designed the parks, the streets, and the parking. He designed at city scale, house scale, room scale.

Another part of my discomfort with the 1967 Manchat project had to do with the attitude it reflected towards the design of public space. In the traditional street and piazza of the Mediterranean vernacular, individual buildings are clearly subordinated t the concept of defining public space. Houses form rows that define the street or form a piazza. Materials don't change whimsically. Each structure has a double role: it is at once a building block of the city as well as a house itself.

There was another shortcoming to the new neighbourhoods of Jerusalem. Although every satellite town had a single master planner with several architects working under his direction, each town turned

Religious ceremonies in one of the courtyards of the Armenian Quarter. *(Joan Almond)*

School children in an Armenian Quarter courtyard. *(Joan Almond)*

The courtyard of the Rockefeller Museum. *(Raffi Magnes Photography)*

The courtyard of the American Colony Hotel. *(Raffi Magnes Photography)*

Hebrew Union College — Model: left foreground, the existing Rau Building; center, the entry and the ceremonial courtyard; right, the reception building and the Library; background, the academic courtyard, and upper left, the residential section of Mamilla.
(Peter Vanderwarker Photographs)

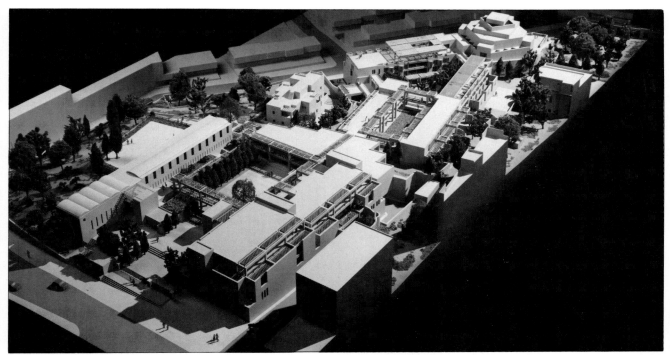

Hebrew Union College — Model showing the interconnection of the various courtyards. From left to right: entrance court, ceremonial court, academic court, youth hostel and upper right, the synagogue. *(Peter Vanderwarker Photographs)*

Hebrew Union College after inauguration.

Hebrew Union College — A place of working and living.

Damascus Gate — The Harvard Fellows' proposal, above a view of the gardens leading to Damascus Gate, below, the arcades with the bus terminal behind them. *(Gene Dyer)*

Yeshivat Porat Yosef — Model of the Yeshiva showing the stone walls containing the compound, the lace-like concrete arches rising above and the translucent and transparent domes.

Yeshivat Porat Yosef — Graffiti on the Yeshiva walls: "Avraham Shrem, return our stolen money and resign immediately."

Yad Vashem Children's Memorial — The reflection of children's faces. *(Raffi Magnes Photographer)*

Yad Vashem Children's Memorial —
Through the natural archway, down the ramp
to the underground chamber.
(Raffi Magnes Photographer)

Yad Vashem Children's Memorial —
The single candle reflecting into infinity.
(Raffi Magnes Photographer)

out to be a grouping of distinct sections separated by traffic arteries. Each of these sections was a world unto itself, with the sense of separation exacerbated by the varied styles. One section forms a fortress-like square with a large central courtyard and gateways at the corners. Another is made of prefabricated panels of triangular cut stone. In another, housing units are shaped into dodecahedrons, piled beehive-like one on top of the other. The imprint of the architect — the architect's notion of what the community should be physically — overwhelms the imprint of the people who live there. Though my 1967 design might have been more cleverly planned than most, it nevertheless extended the design to such a depth that it did not permit the residents to express their own diversity.

There was a sense of uniformity. Was that not also true of the Arab village of Silwan, clearly visible out of my window on the slopes of the Kidron Valley? Yet there was a difference. Silwan was built over a period of sixty or seventy years and each house exhibited the designs of a different person. They had imprinted upon it their uniqueness — a window of strange proportions, a twisted angle, an exuberant grille, a special color. Yet each house was still part of the whole in that each was constructed out of stone.

All this ran through my mind as we sat silently looking at the old drawings. Dan Lansky, my office manager, recalled that the old model was also in the vaults and probably in very bad condition. He suggested we resurrect the model and fix it up for the meeting with ARIM the following week.

I stopped him. "No," I said, "we'd better start again. Let's rethink all of this. Let's create a more open framework for community life, rather than taking the industrial design attitude of solving life down to the last detail. No more placing the toothbrush in the bathroom for people. Let them do that for themselves!"

But ARIM was in a rush. And they didn't want to go through that Via Dolorosa of approvals. I sat there, wondering what to do.

I recalled that the ministry had established a limit of 1500 units for this site — a density of about 8 units per dunam (about 32 units per acre). Why such a high density? Was this land so expensive? Or was land so scarce? Why not 6 units per dunam? Why not 4? Jerusalem is the city of extremes. Ministry housing at 10 dwellings per dunam are a stone's throw away from villages with half that density. I speculated that if we reduced the ministry's density in

Manchat by about half, we could provide small individual lots for most residents.

Each family could get 200 square metres of land. We would just set up a few rules about massing, party walls and relationships between neighbours and let people build their own.

Danny was skeptical. Letting residents build on their own would be much more expensive than using a prefabricated system. (Almost everything being built in the new neighbourhoods is prefabricated.) But I pointed out that contractor-developer profits amount to twenty to thirty percent of the cost of development.

In the Arab sector, for example, there are no large contractors operating at all, nor is any advanced technology being applied. Each family puts up what it can afford on its own small parcel of land. A family might begin with a living room, a bathroom, a single bedroom. A year later when they have a little more money, they may add a room or two, or even a second floor. If a family living on the eighth floor of a prefabricated structure needs more space, all they can do is move to another place.

The Arab family invests its own labour. Walking through the Arab neighbourhoods of Jerusalem on weekends one can often see a father, his sons and relatives putting up a stone wall, connecting plumbing, investing their own "sweat equity." In Jerusalem today, surely investing one's own labour and building in accordance with resources is more meaningful than the apparent economies of mass production.

In the long term I still believe that it is inevitable that high technology, mass production, and automation will be used increasingly in construction. But the long term means decades. In 1967, I believed that within five to ten years we would revolutionize the building industry. But we didn't. We're now in the 1980s and very little in the process of building has changed.

As we talked about reversing much of what we had designed for Manchat in 1967, we were still uneasy about what the results might be. Danny pointed to the self-built suburban developments around Tel Aviv and in other parts of the country where the land was subdivided and given to families. It was like walking through two decades of *House and Home*. There were stuccoed Spanish villas with tiled roofs beside little Swiss chalets with fake timbering over concrete blocks; there were space-ships ready for take-off, conical shapes, free forms, interpenetrating cubes. It was almost like being dropped into an exhibition of giant modern jewellery: white buildings, purple buildings, green buildings — the worst expressions of nouveau riche materialism and pseudo individualism.

The Jewish kitsch of the coastal plain is appropriately balanced by the Arab kitsch of the mountain region. The road from Jerusalem to Ramallah is lined with luxurious villas of every color and material imaginable, usually topped by a giant TV antenna in the shape of the Eiffel Tower.

We began to talk about what would constitute reasonable controls. We had gained some experience from Mamilla and from the controls posed during the reconstruction of the Old City. In Mamilla, our "visual guidelines" expressed in words — no more than one page of double spaced typing — received immediate and unanimous support. So why not do the same with Manchat? Instead of designing individual houses, we would set guidelines for the use of materials — the "syntax" of building.

If someone wanted to built right up to his property line, he had to build a stone wall three metres high. If he wanted to pull back, he had to have a setback of least three metres, and the courtyard thus formed must have a wall around it. Windows and entrances were to be formed as vertical rectangles, reflecting stone construction. Large windows would be built with lintels or arches. Setbacks for roof gardens, positions of gateways and entrances were all defined.

Once we had a set of rules, we played the game of having a couple of architects test the rules, pushing them to the limit by trying to create the ugliest building possible within the rules. In the end we arrived at a set of rules that seemed to work.

What we were attempting to do at Manchat was to develop rules that were concerned with more than just visual unity. Some of the rules affected the relations between houses, and therefore between people. These rules would, in the end, have an immeasurable impact on the kind of life and sense of visual order that would exist in the community. For example, the Israeli energy code required that every house must have solar heating. Left to their own devices, owners might assemble a jumble of collectors of every shape and height. We prescribed that all roofs accommodating collectors be sloped in a southern direction. This pattern created its own vernacular, a roofscape with its own visual unity, an expression of solar orientation

— just as domes or wind vents establish a visual syntax for Arab or Iranian villages.

Two weeks later, taking drawings and a little model, we met with ARIM. The model showed rooms and courtyards and garden walls juxtaposed; the houses were two storeys high at most, but they rose up the hillside five, six and ten storeys, in step with its topography. The project would have the same earthy, village-like feel of the adjacent Arab dwellings, a much more timeless quality than the cleverly manipulated forms of our 1967 scheme.

The people at ARIM first expressed doubt. "Two hundred square metre lots," they said. "It's unheard of. No one would buy lots of less than five hundred square metres. Those who have enough money to build their house want a big piece of land."

"But this is not housing for people who now buy five hundred metre lots!" I told them. "It's for the people who are now buying seventy square metre apartments on the third floor of a four storey walk-up building. If you could deliver this land — even build the periphery walls for them — then they can build seventy square metres for less than it would cost them to buy that much space in a mass-produced building — and they'll have the option of adding another seventy square metres when they have more money in the future."

I suggested that ARIM look at Yemin Moshe, a district built outside the city walls toward the turn of the century by Montefiore and extensively renovated in the 1970s. The houses that were still usable were restored, but many families bought ruins or open lots, perhaps 150 square metres in area, and built traditional townhouses on these tiny parcels. The problems of party walls, coordinating lots with height differences, drainage, and so on were all resolved. Yemin Moshe became one of the most desirable addresses in Jerusalem. People who wanted to live there accepted small lots.

The success of Yemin Moshe created a precedent. It demonstrated how people, given the choice between a tiny lot where they could build their own house and a mass-produced apartment, would opt for the tiny lot.

The ARIM board asked more questions. But in the end, being an adventurous group, they adopted the plan. For me, the idea of parcelling land for individual construction brought things full circle. Manchat reflected the pattern of the villages in and around Jerusalem where Arab families constructed their own dwellings. (Very few "lots" for private houses exist in Jewish parts of Jerusalem.) In Manchat, on a similar scale and in a similar topography, Israeli families would do the same. Considering the attitude of many Israelis towards Arab culture, this was not without its ironies.

Most Israelis have little appreciation for Arab culture. A few sophisticated Jerusalemites now buy Arab embroidery, Palestinian dresses, pottery and copper, or restore an Arab house in a village or in the Old City. But the majority of Israelis dismiss Arab society. Yet on the level of building and urban development, the Arabs certainly demonstrate more responsive and wholesome attitudes.

Consider this: the poor Israeli lives in a housing project apartment built by the ministry. The rich Israeli, with an ever-developing sophistication, now strives to buy an old stone house with all the romanticism of Arab culture, which he can restore. The poor Arab lives in the Muslim Quarter of the Old City or in one of the villages surrounding it. His dream is to get out and live like the Jews do, perhaps in a suburban apartment building. The wealthy Arab who builds his large villa in the northern suburbs of Jerusalem certainly doesn't build anything in the tradition of the Old City. He builds, in the best tradition of Jacques Tati's Mr. Hulot, a concoction of the clichés of modern architecture. But even at that, he would never give up his garden and glazed porch and the compound wall that gives him his privacy.

In other words, even when uncertainty or confusion about style emerges as Arabs westernize and Israelis easternize, the sensitivity of the Arab to amenities in the environment is greater. He is much more reluctant to compromise on that than the Israeli.

In the final analysis, the greatest mystery of urban design is the extent to which people everywhere, east or west, rich or poor, are willing to compromise the quality of their habitat. They shrug, helpless, always believing themselves powerless to influence their environment.

CHAPTER 21

TRANSFORMATION IN TIME

The seed that germinated at the meetings with the Rabbinical Council finally came to fruition in 1980. Three events made it imperative that I produce another working model of the Western Wall.

The first event of significance was a request from the municipality. They wanted to put up a service building (with toilets, first aid, refreshments, tourist information, etc.) by Dung Gate at the edge of the Western Wall precinct. They also decided it was time to restore the historic gate, which the Jordanians had damaged by clumsily widening it.

By 1980, after years of restoration and new construction in the Jewish Quarter, I was naturally reluctant to draw up any plans before the archaeologists had their chance at it. The city agreed and authorized Meir Ben-Dov to excavate. Within ten days he had found the paving of the lower Cardo, or lower Roman main street. It was in excellent shape, with large numbers of stones and a drainage system that was almost intact. The road was just six metres off the alignment that I had fixed for the arcaded street in my Western Wall plan of 1974.

At the same time, the Jerusalem Foundation decided to turn over to the public Benjamin Mazar and Meir Ben-Dov's extensive excavations beside the Temple Mount. They had uncovered some of the columns surrounding the courtyard of the main Umayyad palace and even some of the stone sections of the canal that had been built to irrigate the fruit garden at the centre of the courtyard. I suggested the best way to handle the whole area would be to create an archaeological park. We could restore some elements, remove others to uncover what was underneath, and then landscape with explanatory signs. I further proposed that the Foundation fund the building of a model to show the relationship between the excavation and the rest of the precinct.

Independently of all this, two weeks later we were called upon by the newly appointed director of the Company for the Reconstruction and Development of the Jewish Quarter, Amos Unger, to proceed with the restoration of the buildings on the cliff. He wanted to accommodate two institutions, the Yeshivat Aish Ha Torah (Flame of the Torah) for born-again Jews (secular Jews, mostly from the U.S., who rediscover Orthodoxy) and a building either for the Institute of Biblical Studies, or a youth hostel.

Unger's initiative brought me face to face with the reality that once again events were overtaking my original plan. I was now involved in three ways: with a study model for the archaeological area, with work on the cliff and its buildings, and with the discovery of the lower Cardo. The time had come for me to rethink the whole Western Wall plan.

In the new model I intended to build, I wanted to avoid the static representation of an end product and to devise a method of showing the ever changing process of realization — a dynamic presentation. The model with its many pieces would begin by showing existing conditions. Hidden under would be the layers of archaeological remains. Any new construction would be added as layers on top. Every excavation would bare the archaeology below, each phase an image unto itself. I wanted a model in which, step by step, one could uncover remains, or add buildings, showing the many possible permutations until one reached a final scenario. But each step of the process would be plainly visible as a step in the long process of realization.

The Jerusalem Foundation agreed to pay for a model of the area of the excavations, and Amos Unger commissioned one for the cliff area. Then I thought, why not "donate" the middle and make a new model and a new scheme for the entire precinct?

In a period of three months, model makers reconstructed the history of Jerusalem, layer by layer, all the way up from 1500 B.C. to the existing grade. I spent a half hour with them every day at the workshop in Boston to interpret the photographs and help fill in the gaps where information was missing. We were simply documenting what was there, not yet changing the plan. When all the pieces were in place, I began to make sketches as to how the area should be altered.

The first change to the plan was to shift the arcaded street, which bypassed the praying area connecting Dung Gate with the north-south markets, six metres westward to integrate it with the remnants of the Cardo, thus making its ancient floor the street itself. Second, I decided to preserve the buildings on the cliff and continue their skyline around the northwestern end of the square.

The most exciting discovery had been the Herodian street at the Wall — I now decided to make the street the bottom terrace so that Jews praying at the Wall would stand on the actual stones, at the actual Wall of the Second Temple, exactly as Herod had constructed it. We were able to show the paving of the Herodian walkway stone by stone on the model because we knew the pattern from patches already uncovered.

Around the corner of the Temple Mount on the south side, I proposed that the main Umayyad palace walls, with the courtyard in

the middle, should be built up to their original height. Columns found askew in the courtyard would be put back on their pedestals, and in this central colonnaded courtyard we would restore the traditional Muslim fruit garden with its canals, paved pathways, fruit trees, pomegranates, date palms, and so on.

I wanted the visitor to Jerusalem to find, in the midst of this arid archaeological area, a sudden oasis of fruit trees and jasmine, irrigated by canals as it was some 1300 years ago. I consulted with Nader Ardalan who was able to fill in the details from his studies of Persian and Muslim gardens.

The last element to be redesigned was the Israeli controlled access to the Mughrabi Gate. The temporary steel spiral stairway I had originally proposed to replace the current earth ramp irritated everybody. I redesigned it as a more massive stone structure, ascending almost like a stair in an Escher painting.

The two plans and models (1974 and 1980) were fundamentally the same, but they represented an enormous difference in emphasis. If the "media is the message," then the new model also represented a fundamentally differing approach. The 1974 model was a static representation of a hypothetical final phase to occur fifteen years hence. Everyone, including myself, recognized that the Wall would be subject to many changes generated by changing requirements, attitudes, and particularly archaeological considerations. The model represented only a single vision of many possible ultimate products. Its manner of presentation emphasized new construction and its generating geometry, but played down what already existed on the site. The message was, therefore, that the new order, the Safdie plan, took precedence and superimposed itself on everything that now existed in the precinct.

In contrast, the new model did not give a single representation of a final product. On the contrary, it was made up of over 100 interchangeable pieces, some representing new construction, others archaeological remains or speculations on underlays of archaeology. This meant that there were many permutations of possible end products. I wanted the emphasis to be placed on the possibility of variations — demonstrating the dynamic process that could occur with a large number of variables.

The message of the new model was that the precinct was a transparent layering of past, present and future. It was as if segments of the plans of different periods of Jerusalem — Hasmonean, Herodian, Roman, Byzantine, Umayyad and Mameluke — had been drawn in ink on transparent papers. Overlaid on all that was yet one more layer, the 1980 plan, with its geometry of terraced piazzas and arcaded street. Looking through the sandwich of these plans, one could see glimpses of every period. It was as if someone had immersed the overlaid plans in water, allowing different parts to emerge as ink through the paper, resulting in a montage of past, present and future.

Thus I came to realize for myself the fundamental difference between architecture and urban design and the essential difference in the media each requires.

The new model of the precinct was enormous in size and in cost. The contribution of the Jerusalem Foundation and the Company for the Reconstruction and Development of the Jewish Quarter totalled ten thousand dollars. By the time the workshop had completed it, it had cost almost forty. But I was resigned to the fact that my work in Jerusalem would forever require my own subsidies.

Shortly before the model was completed in July 1982, I met with Teddy Kollek in Jerusalem. I told him how excited I was about the new model of the Wall precinct which was almost ready for shipping. I felt it answered every substantive objection of the Shimron Commission, the archaeologists, the preservationists, even the religious groups. It was a richer plan because it accommodated so much more of the context of the site and because it wove the past and the present more effectively together.

Teddy listened attentively but the notion of bringing the model to Jerusalem made him nervous. He warned me that there were constant conflicts throughout the city with the religious community. He feared this would kindle them once more.

However, both the Jerusalem Foundation and the Company for the Reconstruction and Development of the Jewish Quarter were waiting to see the model. Besides, I had a compulsive urge to get the model to Jerusalem. I felt that its pesence would work magic. It was so compelling, so convincing, that I was sure that anybody who saw it would be completely and immediately persuaded of the beauty and feasibility of the plan.

The model was packed into three crates, each somewhat larger than a coffin. They were too big for Swissair, so they were shipped by the Flying Tigers, who shuttle between New York and Tel Aviv with large cargoes, mostly arms. Nestled among rockets and machine guns sat three coffin-like boxes on their way to Jerusalem.

Looking back on it, I can see that the timing of their arrival was not fortuitous. Tensions between Teddy and the religious parties were at an all-time high. It was August 1982, three weeks after the outcry over the Bronfman amphitheatre. There were demonstrations and violence in the Orthodox neighborhood of Mea Shearim. My name figured heavily as the author of the amphitheatre plan. The Orthodox would seize any occasion to lump me and my plan for the Wall with all their other displeasures with the Kollek administration.

Nonetheless, I was full of optimism about the design. We unpacked the model in my office and I called Teddy and Ruth Cheshin, the director of the Jerusalem Foundation, who arrived with their in-house architect. The model sat on the table with the pieces arranged to show the site's existing condition. For fifteen minutes I went through the act of transformation, placing the new pieces in step by step.

Teddy sat there, at first reserved, then getting redder as his inner tension mounted. Before I could complete the transformation, he shouted, "I told you not to bring it!"

"But Teddy," I protested, "I don't intend to show it to anybody — I'm showing it to you. It's not going to be shown publicly yet."

"You know there are no secrets in this city!" he exclaimed. "Nothing can be hidden here. They're just going to have a heyday!" ("They" meaning the religious parties.) His voice grew louder: "You know the problems we have. You just don't listen. I'm not going to react to this, I'm not even going to look at it. Send it back to the United States. I don't want it in Jerusalem now. It's the wrong time. Good-bye!" And he stormed out of the office.

Ruth Chesin shrugged in embarrassment. She said, "Oh, you know how he is sometimes. He's having a rough time. Be understanding."

That day we packed the model back into its crates and put it in our vault on Mamilla Street.

For five or six days I didn't speak to Teddy. I was hurt and I was playing the part. Then about a week later he called me at home at seven in the morning: "The people from Hebrew Union College were here to see me today. After you presented the final plans to them recently, there was some internal criticism that concerned them. I assured them what a good architect you are and what a contribution you are making to this city. They left very enthusiastic."

So this was his "sulcha." And I thought to myself, Teddy could charm anyone, anytime — he could charm the Ayatolla Khomeini.

The model remains in storage to this very day. From time to time it is uncrated for a special occasion. Once I showed it to Wolf Von Eckardt, architectural critic of *Time* magazine. He was going to write of it as one of the major elements of the rebuilt city. But someone in the Mayor's office heard and it was suggested that though it was indeed an important plan, its time had not yet come, and it was played down in the *Time* piece.

So long as the extreme tensions exist between the religious factions and his own administration, the Mayor will have to be cautious about the plan for the Western Wall. But he cannot stop the developments that continue to go on in and around the site. On the northern edge of the square, the Idra Rabba, a centre for Talmudic Studies which I designed for Rabbi Goren, ex–Chief Ashkenazi Rabbi for Israel, has just been completed. The plans for the Youth Hostel and the Yeshivat Aish Ha Torah have been submitted to the municipal council and approved. Our own improvements to the Dung Gate are under way. But the Mayor and the city often make an effort to minimize my participation as the architect. No sign proclaims that along with Shlomo Aronson I redesigned Dung Gate, nor did we put up a sign when our other works were carried out around the cliffs.

I do believe that my plan for the Wall is the inevitable one. Its main strategy — digging down and placing the praying area at the original level of the Second Temple, the Herodian street — is an idea so powerful that I feel it is inevitable. Such a rich weaving of a past and present, of history and of the future is woven into the designs that I think, indeed believe, the plan will become irresistible.

On the Western Wall, like Mamilla, I've worked for over fifteen years. I know at least twenty more years will be needed to get it finished — given an optimistic scenario of collaboration, the right political circumstances, and a sense of harmony between the various communities in Jerusalem. If I'd started at fifty, I would really be in trouble. Since I started at thirty, I can share in the sense of anticipation.

Tradition has it that when the Messiah comes, the Third Temple will be built. Luckily it is supposed to come down from Heaven already designed. No doubt the Lord has been observing the difficulty of getting architectural plans approved in Jerusalem.

EPILOGUE

1. THE PEOPLE

Mordecai Bentov:

Following a history in the service of both his kibbutz and his country, Bentov died on January 17, 1985, at the age of 84.

Meron Benvenisti:

After departing in 1978 as Deputy Mayor, Benvenisti joined national politics. In the election of 1981, he ran with the Citizens Rights party, a left-of-centre civil liberty oriented party headed by Shulamit Aloni. He was not successful in obtaining a Knesset seat. Following the receipt of a Ph.D. from the Kennedy School of Government at Harvard, Benvenisti became one of the leading world authorities on the economic and social developments of the West Bank. During the 1980s he forecast deteriorating conditions on the West Bank and warned about the irreversibility of the integration of Israel and the West Bank. During the riots and demonstrations which erupted in Gaza and the West Bank at the end of 1987, Benvenisti was one of the most sought after experts by the international media. His book *The Sling and the Club*, published in 1988, is a brilliant analysis of the political choices facing the Israelis and Palestinians in settling their disputes.

Teddy Kollek:

Teddy is about to run for his sixth term as Mayor of Jerusalem. On May 27 of 1988 he turned 77. He emerges from the election in a new political mood. In 1988, the demonstrations in the Gaza Strip and West Bank did not pass over Jerusalem. In February 1988 youths were throwing stones in the city neighbourhoods and for the first time since 1967, there were instances of curfews being imposed on outlying Arab neighborhoods. Polarization was heightened by aggressive acts on both sides. Ariel Sharon moved into a residence in the Moslem Quarter, challenging by his action the status quo. Although the demonstrations of this period harbour the threat of increased polarization and violence in Jerusalem, perhaps they also have within them the potential to impress upon both sides the futility and limitations of the status quo and the need to rethink fundamental relationships, and arrangements.

Amnon Niv:

Following eleven years in the role of City Engineer (Chief City Planner), Amnon Niv withdrew from municipal service to form and head the Jerusalem Center for the Planning of Historic Cities. This institution, established with the support and assistance of Mayor Kollek, is mandated to explore long-term planning and urban design issues in Jerusalem and elsewhere. Amnon Niv hopes to attract commissions and public support for this endeavour.

Eliezer Ronnen:

Having resigned from Karta and having obtained a law degree, Ronnen joined the private sector as a lawyer specializing in real estate development. He was involved in the development of a major shopping centre in the Tel Aviv area and currently remains active in both his private and political endeavours.

Jim Rouse:

Jim Rouse left his position as Chairman of the Board of the Rouse Company of which he was founder.

He later established the Enterprise Foundation and the Enterprise Development Company, which carry out projects in areas of particular social need.

Rabbis Moshe and Avraham Shrem

The rabbis still hold the position of Administrative Director (Avraham) and Academic Director (Moshe) of the yeshiva. However, in 1987, they entered into a serious dispute between themselves over the authority and control of the institution. Each insisted that he could not continue to work with the other and that one of them should withdraw.

The two rabbi brothers have not been on speaking terms for over a year.

In early 1988 the students at the yeshiva stormed into Avraham Shrem's office and destroyed it. They defaced the concrete stone walls of the building with graffiti and posters which read in part:

"Avraham Shrem, stop causing sorrow to the students of wisdom."

"Avraham Shrem, give us back our stolen money and resign immediately."

"Where are the millions of dollars collected, whose whereabouts only you know?"

"Why do you advertise every year and this year that you support 1000 students and 100 rabbis when you do not support us at all?"

Yehuda Tamir:

Shortly after the termination of his tenure as the Chairman of the Company for the Reconstruction and Development of the Jewish Quarter, Yehuda Tamir also left his post as director of the real estate subsidiary of the CLAL group of companies in Israel. He has pursued a career as a developer, active mostly in the construction of projects in Africa and Central America.

Amos Unger:

As the last director of the Company for the Reconstruction and Development of the Jewish Quarter, working with Nissim Abouloff as its chairman, Amos Unger was responsible for the completion of the restoration and rebuilding of that quarter. Under his tenure, he saw to it that the remaining incomplete sectors, archaeological excavations, and infrastructure were completed and opened to the public. In 1987, Amos Unger was appointed as Director General of the Ministry of Construction and Housing. In that capacity, he has taken a personal interest in Mamilla, pressing for the approval of the plan and, finally, directing his Ministry's efforts in the "call for proposal" for developers to construct the project.

Bruno Zevi:

Bruno Zevi continues his activities as author, editor and broadcaster in Rome. In 1987 he was elected to the Italian Parliament.

2. THE PROJECTS

My Office:

Through the 1970s and 1980s, I continued to strive for the same professional standards in my office in Jerusalem as in our offices in Canada and the United States. This was no mean feat considering that professional practice and the building trades in Israel are still evolving and have yet to reach European and American standards.

Several of the architects who apprenticed at the office went on to start their own practice, including two of my office managers, Dan Lansky and Eylon Meromi.

In 1982, a breakthrough in this effort occurred. Uri Shetrit, a young Israeli architect, applied to the Urban Design Program at Harvard. Through a scholarship, he concluded his studies, continuing a two-year apprenticeship in my Boston office. He returned to Jerusalem to lead the office there in what has become a model for local practice. Since then, other architects from the Jerusalem office have come to Harvard to study and apprentice in the Boston office.

Yeshivat Porat Yosef:

After many years of impasse, the rabbis eventually decided to circumvent the arbitrator and negotiate directly with me and our lawyers to try to reach some settlement. After proclaiming for a decade that they did not owe me a cent, a compromise was reached of $250,000, which they began paying in monthly installments to terminate in 1988. Construction was reinitiated. Simultaneously, the classroom wing is being completed and work has begun on dividing the synagogue volume into two rooms, as decided by the arbitrator. The contractor promised that the demolition of the great stone walls surrounding the synagogue would take a couple of months and a few tens of thousands of dollars. But as we suspected, by February of 1988, they had been at it for six months at the cost of hundreds of thousands. Stone by stone, the walls are being demolished with air hammers to accommodate the new arrangement of the two rooms. Stephen Shalom stepped in at one point, threatening to stop the demolition by his own court action. He was dissuaded from doing so by the Minister of Housing, David Levy, who felt that such an open rift in the Sephardic community was not acceptable. Shalom withdrew his threatened action. For myself, I was resigned that the Great Synagogue was simply not to be and proceeded to cooperate with the change. I continue to hope that they will be able to gather enough funds to eventually complete the building once and for all.

Mamilla:

After years of additional deliberation, everyone concerned (the Minister of Construction and Housing, David Levy, the Municipality of Jerusalem, the Ministry of Finance and all the public approving authorities) got behind the implementation of Mamilla. By the end of 1987 the plan had been fully approved. It was enacted into law following public deposition and public hearings. In August 1987 Karta and its new chairman, Nissim Aboulloff (also the chairman of the Company for the Reconstruction and Development of the Jewish Quarter) called for proposals of developers to implement the project. Over fifty applied and three were selected to the short list of those to enter final negotiations. Amos Unger, now Director General of the Ministry of Construction and Housing, helped to steward the plan to fruition. In June of 1988, David Levy, Amos Unger and Nissim Aboulloff travelled to London to meet with Cyril Stein, chairman of the Ladbroke Group. On March 29, 1989, a contract was signed designating Ladbroke as the developer for all of Mamilla. Ladbroke, in turn, has engaged my office as architect for the implementation of the project. Exactly sixteen years after I was first commissioned to draw the plans, Mamilla proceeds to realization.

The Western Wall:

A succession of coalition governments, including the National Unity government in which the religious parties had a decisive balancing role, made it impossible for any progress to be made at the political front. In the meantime, small compromises were being made on the site. The small service building, with shops and conveniences by Dung Gate which I had designed, was redesigned by Amnon Niv, the City Engineer, with the explanation that my participation so irritates the religious community that it would impede progress. Similarly, a series of ramps leading from Dung Gate to the Wall, as proposed in my plan, were detailed for construction by Hillel Schocken, the architect for the Jerusalem Foundation. While the gesture of linking the levels of Dung Gate with the Wall more closely as proposed by my plan was fulfilled, the details of Schocken's plan left much to be desired.

From time to time the great model, with its hundreds of pieces, is unveiled. Someone sees it afresh and the flame is rekindled. Visitors from abroad, sometimes political leaders, have been mesmerized by it. I have learned from Mamilla to lie low and wait for the right moment. I hope that the moment of the Western Wall plan will come.

Manchat:

In early 1988, the revised plan incorporating the idea of small parcels of land was formally approved and moved on to realization. Twenty-one years after the first plan was drawn under the auspices of the Minister of Housing, Mordechai Bentov, construction is about to begin on the site.

Hebrew Union College:

The campus opened with great excitement in the fall of 1986. Construction continued on the library, which was inaugurated in March 1988. The Hebrew Union College campus has become a lively, vital place for Jerusalem's cultural and social life. The court-yards are intense with activity. The Youth Hostel (Beit Shmuel Guest House), run by the World Union for Progressive Judaism under the leadership of Rabbi Dick Hirsch, has drawn both the young and the old to its diverse activities: seminars, lectures, folk singing, concerts, Friday night welcoming of the Sabbath, weddings, bar mitzvahs and receptions. In 1984, I embarked upon yet another venture with the Hebrew Union College by accepting the commission to design the Hebrew Union College Center for American Jewish Life and Skirball Museum in Los Angeles.

The Jewish Quarter:

With the exception of the parking garage, all work in the Jewish Quarter was completed by 1987 and it has settled into "normal life." Yehuda Tamir's hopes for an integrated and mixed community of secular and Orthodox Jews, manifested in his home sale policy, have not been realized. Through the market forces and slow evolution, the Jewish Quarter has become almost exclusively Orthodox. Most secular residents have found the environment increasingly alienating. As they moved out, their residences were purchased by Orthodox Jews.

The Jewish Quarter continues to be a rather isolated neighbourhood, having little interaction with the surrounding quarters of the Old City or with its principal markets. Shops, banks and other services within the quarter provide for its population, who rarely cross over to the market, where all of these are generally available.

The Jewish Quarter has become a major tourist attraction.

The upper Cardo, running parallel to the Street of the Jews, opened to the public in 1986 along with the shops fronting on it. The many archaeological remnants — the First Temple Wall, the Herodian buildings under Yeshivat HaKotel and Porat Yosef, and scores of other finds have been cleaned up, restored, and supplemented by lighting and explanatory text and good signage. They offer the tourists an underground city: a journey of exploration to the history of Jerusalem.

3. THE MOSAIC

As Teddy Kollek puts it, Jerusalem is not a melting pot, but a mosaic of cultures, peoples, and religions. As such it must be the richest city in the world. Inside the Old City walls are the Ethiopians, the Greek Orthodox, the Armenians, the Muslims, the religious Jews. Outside the walls are the Greek colony, the American colony, the Russian compound, the Bukharian Quarter, and dozens more. I believe this multilingual, multiracial, multireligious aspect must be preserved.

Coexistence between Jewish groups causes as many problems as between Arab and Jew. A secular Jew is quite likely to have a party on Friday evening (the beginning of the Sabbath), or play his radio loudly, or do any of a number of things a religious Jew would find distasteful or unacceptable. Thus, neighbourhoods all over Jerusalem are very homogeneous — not just Arabs keeping to themselves, but oriental Jews living apart from the European Jews, religious Jews from secular Jews.

After one has been here for some time, one comes to understand that the people of this city prefer to remain in their own enclaves. The Armenians want to speak Armenian. They want to go to Armenian shops, to have their seminary and church and school right next to them. They don't want Muslims in their midst who have different lifestyles — who fast on Ramadan and whose muezzin roar out at four in the morning. It is the same for the Muslims and for the eastern and western, secular and Orthodox Jews. Each group wants its own little world and culture.

Yet each group is part of a greater city. Life in that city also involves interacting with the others in continuous daily activities: in the marketplace, in the business world.

Everyone watches films, but the languages differ. Everyone listens to concerts — but sometimes the music is Arab, sometimes it is western. Everybody loves sports. And we certainly all do business together, so there is that inescapable setting for interaction.

Whenever the city mosaic is woven together to form physical points of junction, that is where the communal life of the greater community of Jerusalem takes place.

Jerusalem is a world city. Yet is also the capital of Israel. Certain factions of Israeli society want to Judaize — to increase the Jewish presence — at the expense of others in the city. I believe this must be strongly resisted. It would eventually destroy Jerusalem as a world city, and I say that not just as a humanist, but as an urbanist and an Israeli. When the city was divided, each half was an intolerably parochial place. For Jerusalem to survive as a unique place in the world, the conditions for the spiritual, economic, and social growth of these groups must be protected.

I believe that, left to themselves and with little external intervention, the people of the city will eventually opt for a community which is truly undivided. The sense of a cohesively functioning metropolis is a desire shared by the people of Jerusalem. This commitment to bring people together is based on the hope that notwithstanding its bloody history of wars and conquest, Jerusalem might become an example of the ability of very different peoples to live and work together in peace. There are seeds of that harmony today. That is the vision of the city I am trying to communicate and to build for. To achieve this we must create places of meeting. Every act of planning and building must strive towards this end.

INDEX